# MINDFUL OF HORSES

HELEN CHERRY

**BALBOA.**PRESS

A DIVISION OF HAY HOUSE

Balboa Press books may be ordered through booksellers or by contacting:

Balboa Press
A Division of Hay House
1663 Liberty Drive
Bloomington, IN 47403
www.balboapress.co.uk
UK TFN: 0800 0148647 (Toll Free inside the UK)
UK Local: 02036 956325 (+44 20 3695 6325 from outside the UK)

Print information available on the last page.

ISBN: 978-1-9822-8333-9 (sc)
ISBN: 978-1-9822-8335-3 (hc)
ISBN: 978-1-9822-8334-6 (e)

Balboa Press rev. date: 03/08/2021

This book is dedicated to Nancy, Jacko, and Nadur.

I thank you from the bottom of my heart
for guiding me towards the light.

# CONTENTS

# ACKNOWLEDGEMENTS

As this was my first foray into the world of writing, I want to thank some wonderful people for their help and support. My dear friend Sara K, for not only attending the life writing course with me but also reading the book, giving your honest appraisal, and giving of your time to help me reorganise the manuscript. Thank you to Sara Withy and Jon Bennett, for your immense support and honesty and for encouraging me to see it through. I appreciate enormously the enthusiasm, creativity, and talent of Carolyn Tyrer in her painting which serves as the beautiful book cover.

Last but by no means least I thank my extraordinary daughter, who has stood by my side not only throughout this process but also through the experiences that create the content of the book. You never judge me or waver in your love or your support for me. You fly so high that you continue to amaze and inspire me. I love you dearly.

# INTRODUCTION

We stood there looking at each other. She was this most delicious chocolate-brown bay mare, beautifully blanket-clipped with a crazy white flash down her nose like a strip of lightning. Nomadic Nancy was her name, and I had no idea as we looked at each other that she would take me on a life-changing journey. Those beautiful gentle eyes of hers looked at me, peering right into me as if she knew me, as if she had been waiting for me. In that gentle, quiet moment I knew we would be together, because this wasn't the first time this had happened. Jacko had been standing at the back of a small, dark stable the first time I met him years earlier. He was covered in mud, his mane stuck up like a silver Mohican from poll to withers as he was happily munching his hay. When I looked over the stable door, he nonchalantly turned to look at me and sighed as if to say, *Finally, you're here.* I knew in that instant that he was coming home with me. I remember flashing a toothy smile and saying out loud, "You'll do." He was jolly, talented, and so much fun that I couldn't help but smile and feel happy around him. Jacko carried me through my divorce and the hardest times I've ever faced, bringing joy into my life at a time when everything had fallen apart and I was balancing precariously on the fence between sanity and mental despair. He became the rock that held me up and kept me moving forward. He is also the horse that made me aware of the profound and gentle power of equine healing, as he helped traumatised children find their voices.

Nancy joined us and settled in well, but very quickly I became aware there was something wrong with her. In my determined quest to help heal her, the journey ventured into realms of healing I had no idea existed. I had my eyes and mind opened to many unusual and wonderful things. All along, however, the biggest change was happening to me in a very organic way, changing my life forever without my even realising it. I honestly thought I was healing her, but in fact Nancy healed *my* life. She gave me focus, a new career, and a new confidence to walk my own path. She helped me to find *me* again. She drove me to discover who I could be and to believe in what I could do.

Nancy and Jacko were my guides on an incredible path of healing and life changes that inspired this book. But the story doesn't finish with them. Nancy gifted me a colt foal whom I named Nadur. He continues the journey, refining me as a horsewoman and teaching me a greater self-awareness and lightness. More extraordinary, though, is his ability to help me see the self-limiting beliefs and behaviours I have unwittingly developed during my life. I have had to delve into the scary world of self with Nadur. He mirrors the behavioural patterns I had adopted to survive but no longer need. I have no idea I am using them until he shows me. He challenges me to address these all the time, and by doing so, he demands that my better self emerge. He has connected my mind to my body; this is without a doubt the hardest part of my journey. With Nancy, I didn't realise she was healing me, whereas with Nadur, I am fully aware of and participating in the changes he facilitates. He is extremely sensitive and has taught me a much deeper understanding of being mindful and what true softness really means. Not just in our relationship but also in a way that entwines itself into my whole life. He raises the bar regularly and demands that I reach for it.

This book is about a journey that began without my realising I needed it. It is about mental health as much as it is about these three wonderful horses playing their very different roles: driving me on, carrying me, and teaching me. It has not been easy; change seldom is, I guess. My subconscious tried hard to sabotage my every turn, but guided by my horses as I followed the breadcrumbs they laid, I learned the right lessons at the right time. Ultimately, I learned why my brain had been conditioned the way it was to repeat negative patterns over and over. I was then able to take that leap of faith, stepping out of comfortable and into extraordinary!

Along the way, I have read many inspiring books, met and learned from some truly gifted people, and made some wonderful friends. I experienced unusual events, revisited past experiences, and had many a light-bulb moment. I have taken control of my mind. I restructured my brain and my beliefs, and now I understand the power I have to change anything in my life that doesn't fit.

I still love the thrill of riding horses, but I look at them as so much more than transportation and sport. My horses have been my guides, my teachers, my healers. I am filled with gratitude that they chose to be part of my life.

# CHAPTER 1

# NANCY

I felt the horse beneath me freeze for a moment and then shudder, as a powerful wave of energy surged through her body. I knew it wasn't good. This was going to hurt. She launched herself so fast and so high up into the air that my vision blurred. One second I was looking at her ears, and the next second I was looking at the sky with her front legs high above us, and then at her back with the saddle coming down on top of me. Everything had happened lightning fast then momentarily went slow motion. I remember having time to think, *I don't want my daughter to see me crushed.*

Somehow I found purchase against some part of her. Fuelled with adrenalin, I pushed with all my might. *Crunch!* Then quiet! Then screaming! That's what I heard as I lay in the grass gasping in pain. A tangle of human and horse, bodies, legs, and leather tack. She had flipped right up and over. I was now partly underneath a panicked horse that was screaming and scrambling about, trying to get up.

A few months ago I'd had a choice to make: buy this highly strung five-year-old thoroughbred mare that had little education or experience, who was clipped, shod, and high maintenance, or buy the solid twelve-year-old Irish mare who had been there, had done it, and could live out twenty-four-seven unshod, unrugged, and uncomplicated? Now, my rational brain was clearly rooting for the Irish mare. I needed something I could ride out with my young daughter, who was now riding my beloved Jacko, a 14.2 hands Irish sports pony who could turn his hoof to anything. My daughter had outgrown her awesome little pony Toto (short for "Totally Amazing", which he truly was). Jacko was now her teacher.

So I needed an equine companion to accompany them on fun rides, riding with the bloodhounds and generally gallivanting around the countryside to escape from my real life. So of course I bought Nancy, the five-year-old thoroughbred. I had to, really, because no matter how much my rational brain argued with my heart, Nancy had stood there with those beautiful gentle eyes and had looked right into my soul. It was one of those moments when I just knew in my heart we had to be together.

Nancy came home with me to live with Jacko and our other horses becoming a much-loved member of our herd. But very quickly it became clear that something was wrong. She would evade being tacked up, making it very difficult to put the bridle and saddle on, albeit in a quietly defiant but gentle way. She would also nip me with her lips, not her teeth, when I got the saddle on and tried adjusting it. When she was tacked up, she behaved impeccably; she was genuinely a very sweet horse who was eager to please.

However, she felt ever so slightly lame to me every time I rode her. She would also very politely stop when going down a hill. All these little things were just not normal for a horse to do if it was happy and comfortable. I had the saddle fitter out, and I also asked more-experienced trainers to look at her to see if she looked or felt lame to them. She looked sound. There was no problem with her saddle either, but my gut was still telling me there was something wrong. Over the next few months, her teeth were checked, the farrier visited regularly, and the vets checked her over. I had every conceivable modality of equine therapist out to check over her musculoskeletal structure. It cost a small fortune. All of them told me she was fine and that they couldn't find anything wrong with her. So, crack on, as they would say. Which is what I did. In my ignorance, and in my belief that these professionals knew more than I did, I went against my gut instinct. I did crack on.

It was whilst I was lying in the grass, really hurting after Nancy had finally exploded underneath me, that I wished I had listened to my gut. She had just launched into the air as if she had no other option. Bits of tack had gone everywhere, and luckily the safety stirrups I had on had done their job and came off when I pushed away with all my might, instead of trapping me. It all had happened so fast that my daughter, who was riding in front of me on Jacko, didn't see any of it. She just heard a noise. And when she turned, we were already upside down, tangled in a heap in the grass and mud. It was a horrid mess.

For a horse to throw itself over backwards with complete disregard for its own safety and well-being is very rare. It usually indicates a serious problem, either physical or mental. Although I did come out of it—for the most part—unbroken, just battered, badly bruised, and torn, I never wanted to see that look of abject distress on a horse's face ever again, let alone hear a horse screaming and know I had caused it. This horse pulled the most awful faces, snorting and puffing, with sweat pouring off her. She just didn't know what to do with herself. Clearly she was in great pain, but at the same time I had this overwhelming feeling that she was also very distressed at what she had just done.

This was out of character for such a polite, gentle, and willing-to-please little mare, so I kept telling her over and over that it was OK, that I was OK, and that I was to blame. I had known deep down that something was not right with her, but instead of trusting my gut feeling, I had listened to others. I felt so ashamed of myself. I promised her there and then that I would find a way to help her. I promised to go and learn and that I would try anything to find a way to understand. No matter what, I would get to the bottom of this. I swore to myself as much as to Nancy that I would never be the cause of such pain and distress again, *ever*.

3

# CHAPTER 2

# ROSE-TINTED GLASSES

———— ❧ ————

I had been married for eleven years at this time. My very energetic, intelligent young daughter of eight, who also loved riding amongst a whole swath of other interests, was a joy to her mother. We spent a lot of time riding together and laughing at all the antics our mounts got up to. Jacko was fifteen years old when he came into my life in 2006. He had spent two years recovering from an accident that had seen him gallop out onto a main road and hit and roll over a car.

He needed so much time to recover, and his young rider couldn't wait that long to continue her jumping career, so she bought another horse and put Jacko up for sale. I was the lucky human who got to take him home. From the moment I met him, I knew with my whole being that he was special. I smiled the biggest smile the moment I saw him, as if my body recognised him. He was pure cheeky fun and joy wrapped up in a fabulous bay roan body with a brown head and silvery grey mane and tail. He also had the shape of a white heart on his forehead. And half his right nostril was missing.

In the two years I had owned him, we had had so many fun times, so much laughter. My daughter on her fabulous Toto and me on Jacko—we could do anything with these talented little horses. I felt invincible, free, and safe. He came just at a time when my rose-tinted glasses were falling off and I was beginning to see my life, and particularly my marriage, in a whole new light.

Back in 2002, I had started a business that sold local food produced within a fifty-mile radius of the shop. This had come about because the pilot farmers' markets at which I had been selling my own home-produced lamb were such a success. Customers were wanting to buy all the produce they found at the farmers' markets every day, not just once a month. I opened the shop and—boom—it just took off. I became very busy very quickly. In the first few years I juggled motherhood and the demands of this successful new venture fairly well, I thought.

However, it soon became apparent that as the business became a much bigger thing than expected, quicker than expected, I needed help. My husband left his job and joined the business. But it wasn't long before I noticed I was experiencing patterns within our relationship that I had experienced before but thought we'd left behind. I guess I didn't really want to face the truth of it at first, so I just buried my head and tried to ignore what I was experiencing, telling myself, *It's probably nothing. Don't be so silly.* It was little things at first, such as the fact that he was not really listening to me, and then taking over. And he was ignoring my wishes and my opinions on business matters, or so it seemed.

I would reason that as a new mother with a full-on business, I was probably overstressed and misreading the situation. So I made excuses to myself about why I should ignore this nagging feeling of unease and just carry on. Then my husband's familiar pattern that had reared its head in previous ventures, of putting everyone else's demands or needs before our own, began to surface. This was harder to ignore, as it wasn't just at work, but it interrupted our family life too. Not wanting to admit it, though, I purposely avoided thinking about it.

Jacko carried me through these confusing times and somehow always made me smile. I could ignore reality whilst with him, keeping my head buried firmly in the sand. I always left his company feeling calmer and somehow back in control. He had, without a doubt, become my rock, as slowly everything else began to crumble. For the next three years, Jacko was my escape from the unease and pending crash. The discontent that had occurred between my husband and me in our working adventures was getting so obvious now that it was hard to ignore. And then negative patterns I had noticed before in our private life began to resurface. Although I tried to ignore them, finally things got so bad that I couldn't pull the wool over my own eyes any longer. The business was expanding quickly, and to me it felt like it was all a little too fast, getting out of control, but my husband wanted to push on. He involved a financial partner and attempted to amalgamate with another local business. I sat in meetings feeling more and more like an extra in a movie, and increasingly I felt like I had no voice. I didn't want this amalgamation. My husband and his new partner systematically went through the motions of looking like they were listening to my opinions, only to display a monumental lack of empathy towards me afterwards, completely ignoring me. I didn't have a voice, it seemed. I couldn't make myself be heard. And then I realised that when the chips were down and I needed my husband to be there for me and to support me, he was *not* and did not. He sat there once in silence whilst I was grilled by our partner for not putting our daughter into nursery full-time to give my full attention to the business. There was no way I was going to do that. I wanted to be part of her life and loved the experience of being a mum to her. I wasn't going to miss out on her growing up just for the sake of expanding the bloody business. As far as I was concerned, family was a priority. As I looked to my husband for support in this, he just looked away as if it had nothing to do with him. That was the day I realised I was on my own, and the rose-tinted glasses I had tried so hard to keep firmly in place finally fell off. He didn't stand up and fight in my corner with me. He didn't stand up and say that

I was the one who had started that bloody business and that most evenings, once our daughter was in bed, I worked into the night doing extra paperwork and other jobs for the business. I more than pulled my weight; I juggled business duties, family duties, and all the housework. I couldn't believe what was happening. I was definitely on my own, and I was numb with the realisation. I hadn't wanted to see it before, but it was there all along; this was just the final nail. My sixth sense was also in full alert at this time, flagging up the possibility that I was not the only woman in his life. We just know these things sometimes, but again I didn't really want to admit it. I remember a few days later I discussed very frankly with him the fact that it was either the business or our marriage that was going down. We couldn't go on as we were; I couldn't go on like that. He nodded in all the right places; he commented on things at the right time; and for all intents and purposes he seemed now to have a grasp of the seriousness of where we were and how I really felt. The following day, though, off he went to work, acting as if the conversation had never taken place. I was stunned. When I confronted him about making a decision about it, or at least making changes, he just smiled at me and told me, "Don't be so dramatic. It really isn't that bad." *Crash!* I was done!

CHAPTER 3

# ENERGY

I was wrecked, and I needed to escape—or at the least I realised I needed to change just one thing. So, in 2008 I left the business, leaving my husband in charge, and took up a job at a thoroughbred stud farm. I was still hopeful at this point, as I tried desperately to cling to the rose-tinted glasses just a little longer, that having at least a breather from each other during the working day would perhaps allow my husband and me to restore some part of us. At the very least, it meant I had time out to try to get my head straight. Perhaps things weren't as bad as they seemed?

The owner of the stud farm, a very knowledgeable horsewoman called Ellie Wright, upon hearing about Nancy, suggested that I contact her friend. The friend was a human reiki healer who would also work with horses. I had no idea what reiki was, but I was up for trying anything that might help. And I trusted Ellie, the fountain of knowledge that she was.

So the date was upon us for the reiki healer to arrive. Nancy was in her stable, waiting. I didn't know what to expect, so I had groomed her to a gleaming softness in readiness and given her hay to feast on. As the reiki session got under way and the woman stood there not touching Nancy and not seemingly doing anything, I did wonder if I had once again just paid yet another professional a large sum of money for nothing. What the hell was going on?! *Why isn't she doing anything?* I thought. I tried to stop judging this woman, whom I had all my hopes pinned on, and took a deep breath. Keeping quiet, I decided to watch Nancy instead. She looked so peaceful now that I soon forgot my internal rantings, noting that her head had lowered, her body looked softer and more relaxed, and her eyes appeared sleepy. For the first time since the incident, Nancy looked calm and really, truly relaxed. I was also feeling relaxed and enjoying this quiet and peace. About twenty minutes had passed, when Nancy suddenly opened her eyes and looked straight at me. I heard a voice, clear as day, say, "Thank you."

Before I even thought about it, I smiled and said out loud, "You are very welcome."

The reiki woman turned to me and said, "Oh, you heard her too?" as she had also said "You are very welcome" out loud at the exact same time as I had. I looked at her in complete shock as I realised she meant it was Nancy whom we had just heard saying "thank you". I just smiled at her and pretended it was all perfectly normal. Inside, however, my mind was racing. One minute I was telling myself not to be so bloody stupid—of course I hadn't just heard Nancy talk—and the next minute I was so excited that I wanted to run outside and laugh and shout it to the world. How bloody awesome! I had just heard my horse talk!

The session lasted for about an hour. Nancy was left in such a relaxed state that I was thrilled for her. However, I still didn't understand what reiki was, and I had no clear answers as to what was wrong with my horse. Where was her pain? The reiki woman couldn't offer any insight into what was going on, but she was the only therapist who had been able to comfort Nancy and help her relax. My question now was, "What is it about reiki that has facilitated this relaxation and the hearing of my horse's voice?"

Now, I had worked with horses a lot, and in several countries too, and I had had the pleasure of connecting with one of these horses on a level I had never experienced before or since. Sailor was a stock horse in the Queensland outback of Australia. Whilst I was jillarooing (basically an Aussie term for a female farmhand) on a forty-eight-thousand-acre sheep and cattle station, he had been my partner for eight to nine hours a day, every day for weeks. It was just him and me, the heat and the dust, along with the masses of wild birds and kangaroos to keep us company. We mustered sheep and cattle together, covering thousands of acres. We would stop and drink together. We ate together, swam together, and literally became so in tune with each other that I only needed to think something and he was doing it. Equally, I seemed to know intuitively when Sailor needed to find water or rest. It was easy, comfortable, and completely natural. I have so many wonderful memories of that time. Sailor looked after me so well that I almost didn't come home to England. I felt completely at home out there in the middle of thousands of acres of nothing with him at my side. The land was alive and buzzing with a quiet natural rhythm that was comforting in the vastness of the landscape. And although I never heard him "talk" to me, I could relate to being so in tune with another species that we could communicate in a fashion with thought alone.

So I decided to enrol on a reiki course to learn and understand two things primarily: (1) how to help Nancy into that very visible state of utter relaxation and calmness she so clearly enjoyed and probably needed more of and (2) how to discover how I could have actually heard my horse say "thank you".

It was a whole new world I found myself being immersed in. I can only describe it as a revelation to be with people who imbued gentleness and calm and interacted with all living things in a quiet, respectful manner. It was like stepping off the conveyor belt of my hectic, noisy, unhappy life into a calmness which allowed me to take a deep breath and sigh. Then I would feel my whole being as alive and, for the first time, would look inside myself, within my mind and my body, and take note of what it felt like. This I had never done before—had never even thought of doing it before. I would stop, relax, and then begin to sense the flow of energy. Then I would turn my attention towards feeling the energy of other beings too, feeling the energy around them and pulsing from them. It was wondrous and fun as we played around with the tasks we had been set with, helping us to develop this feel. I began to learn how to be a conduit for the universal energy that flows through all living things. I encountered my hands heating up during one task and then feeling my legs tingling and vibrating when being a guinea pig for the other students to practise on. It was peculiar and enlightening, and I really enjoyed it. I could see why Nancy had fallen into a sleepy trance. My course was being held in a log cabin at the end of the reiki master's garden. I must say that I didn't really want to leave it. The feeling of wellness and aliveness that the course had opened up in me was contagious. I didn't want to lose it when I stepped back into my real world. However it was just a two-day course (Shoden— Level 1 Reiki), and it did have to end, albeit rather too quickly. So I drove straight back to Nancy's stable, convinced that I would see her fall into that trance-like state I had witnessed. I stood next to her and practised what I had learned, expecting any minute to see her demeanour change. I emptied my mind of thoughts and chatter and just focused on the flow of energy from my crown through my body and out to my hands. I wasn't drawn to any particular part of her body, and I couldn't really feel the energy either now, which was weird. I must have stood there for thirty minutes or so trying my hardest, wishing for the outcome I had hoped for. However, this was not to be. I was clearly rubbish at this, and although I had understood the theory of energy healing and had actually felt the energy whilst on my course, it was not happening quite the way I had imagined today! Nancy looked at me. I apologised to her for my inadequacy as I slumped down on an upturned bucket opposite her, feeling quite pathetic. I had so hoped to be able to give her some comfort. Whilst I was deep in thought about where I may be going wrong, thinking that maybe I was trying too hard, I heard Nancy walk over to me. She then balanced her nose on top of my head and just stood there, her touch and gentleness feeling really comforting. Not moving, I just sat there with the weight of her soft squashy nose on my head, enjoying this warm contact with her. It was a lovely thing. We must have stayed like that for a few minutes, just being in the moment, before she stepped to my left and lay down. She curled right up into a foetus shape in the deep straw bed next to me just like a dog would. I was just starting to think that I had never seen a horse do that when I was hit by this consuming wave of grief like nothing I had ever felt before. I burst into tears and sat there sobbing, the tears uncontrollably rolling down my face. In that instant, I was hit with the knowledge that Nancy had given birth to a filly foal that had been taken away from her really young, and my goodness, I felt her pain and anguish. The consuming devastation of loss was unbearable. I had this whole story in my head instantly in picture form, and I knew the grief and the despair were hers. Nancy was showing me how she felt and what had happened. I knew it without a doubt in my mind, and it scared the hell out of me. How could she do that? How could I see that and understand that about her? This was not normal. In my mind-blown fright, I stroked her neck, apologised, and scrambled out of the stable as quickly as I could. As I drove home in shock, still crying and feeling absolute despair, I reasoned that I was truly losing my mind. The stress of my personal situation at this time was clearly unravelling me and must have been the cause of this weird experience. However, I couldn't ignore the consuming depth of that gut-wrenching grief I had felt, and I also couldn't stop seeing the very clear pictures of the filly foal I had seen in my mind. As a mother of a beautiful young girl myself, I could empathise. And I couldn't bear the thought of Nancy suffering the loss of her baby alone. If these were actually her feelings, then I needed to help her. So, true to character, I started to study. The first thing to do was to contact the stud farm that had bred her and try to find out as much info about Nancy as possible. That was to be the second massive shock I had. I held the phone to my ear in stunned silence as the lovely woman on the other end of the line told me quite happily that, yes, she remembered Nomadic Nancy; Nancy had been sold with a beautiful filly foal at foot when Nancy was about three years old. OMG!

Up until then, I had had no idea that Nancy had even had a foal, let alone a filly foal. So it was true then; the pictures and story I had witnessed from Nancy that day in the stable were all hers. As if opening my mind to the wonderful world of energy healing wasn't a big enough shock, this interspecies communication was really pushing at the boundaries of my belief system. I followed the trail of Nancy's ownership a little further, but the next owner was not so forthcoming and quickly made his excuses when I asked about the foal and also if there had been any incidents or accidents that he could recall whilst he knew her.

In most horse establishments, it's not uncommon for foals to be weaned early at six months of age, which may have accounted for Nancy's emotional grief, but I got the feeling that this filly had been taken away earlier than that. With regards to the incident, the man had become a little defensive and vague, even though I explained that I wasn't looking for monetary compensation or a person to blame; I just wanted to get to the bottom of her problems and understand what may be causing her physical pain and her emotional pain. He clearly thought I was some crazy woman out to trap him somehow, so there was nothing more to be gained from this avenue of information. I drew a blank as to where Nancy had gone next or what had happened to the filly foal, and was left feeling frustrated at the thought of poor Nancy living with that grief as well as the physical pain. I still didn't know how to help her or how interspecies communication actually occurs.

The reiki, however, was having another effect, not on Nancy, but on me. I was determined to keep practising. We had all been given some homework on the course which was all about self-healing work. I would find short snaps of time to practise the meditations and mindfulness precepts that our reiki master had shared with us, and I was beginning to look forward to them. At the beginning, it was kind of a nuisance to (1) find the time and (2) switch off the turmoil in my mind enough to do them. As with any skill, practice makes perfect, so I made myself allot time each day. However, over the weeks I began to realise that I actually looked forward to those quiet moments more than anything and that I was able to focus on my breathing, calm my mind, and enjoy just being in that state. Those moments became like jewels of still, calm water amidst a stormy sea. I revelled in them.

# CHAPTER 4

# COMMUNICATION

I did continue to practise my reiki prowess. Not very successfully, I might add, but I also decided to enrol on two other courses at this time in an attempt to further understand what I was experiencing with Nancy. I hoped to find a way to help her. The first of these was a weekend course in animal communication. I hadn't known such a thing even existed a few weeks ago and had no intention of becoming Dr Doolittle, but I did hope to come away understanding how communication with another species occurs. I will admit that I was Mrs Sceptical before I walked into the meeting room, but then upon opening the door to find another course participant walking about the room, wafting burning sage around and chanting a cleansing spell, well, this was too much! This woman then turned to me as I sat down and exclaimed, "What a beautiful aura you have," sitting herself down next to me and smiling. Internally a battle royale was taking place as now the urge to get up and leave was monumentally strong. *They are quite mad!* I thought. But I was here for Nancy, not me, so I stayed firmly seated in the chair and tried not to engage in conversation with this obviously crazy woman.

I was not prepared for the things I learned during the weekend or for how I myself was able to accurately pick up on information and tune into not only horses on-site but also pictures of animals that we had all been asked to bring with us. The one picture that will always stand out to me was of an elderly dog looking at the camera. All the photos we had brought had been put face down on the table and shuffled, so we had no idea who had brought which photo. We were then asked to pick one up, and then we had ten minutes to write down anything and everything that popped into our heads upon looking at the photo. As soon as I picked up the picture of the elderly dog and looked at it, I knew the dog was dead. OMG, how was I supposed to announce that? Supposing the dog hadn't been dead when the person who knew it had left for the course this morning? Or if it wasn't dead at all, as I really expected, how awful and horrid would I look? I continued to scribble down all that popped into my head, which included the fact that this dog worked with his nose a lot! *No shit, Sherlock,* I thought. *It's a dog; of course it uses its nose!* OK, so I was panicking a little as not only was I sitting there having a chat with a photo of a dead dog but also it was now my turn to tell all. So on the premise that I would never have to see these people again if they thought badly of me, I decided to just blurt it out: "This dog is no longer with us, but he did use his nose a lot when he was alive," I said, blushing furiously and waiting for the gasps of horror. Unbeknown to me, the picture belonged to—yes, you guessed it— the crazy sage-burning woman! She looked at me and burst into tears, muttering through her sniffles and snorts that *yes,* indeed the dog was dead. She then went on to say, to my utter surprise, that he had been a sniffer dog with the police and had worked with her dad. *Wow!* I should have felt very happy and relieved, and quite chuffed at my talents for animal communication, but actually all I wanted to do was punch her in the face for the awful position she had put me in. I mean, who brings a picture of a dead dog to a course? *How unfair and unthoughtful!* I thought. I had to sit on my hands and put a smile on my face and was thankful it was an animal communication course and not a human telepathy course.

With my limited mindset and knowledge at that time in my life, I imagined the weekend would be firmly placed in the category of completely bonkers things I've done. But that course, albeit short, had given me the means to understand how I may have been able to receive pictures and feelings from Nancy. With the combination of the course and the reiki weekend, I was beginning to understand that we are energy—everything is vibrating energy. Thoughts and emotions are energy, as are the physiological tissues of our bodies, all vibrating at different frequencies. By calming my thoughts, emptying my mind of chatter, and practising to be quietly present, aware, and receptive, I found it is possible to change the frequency with which my mind vibrates to align with the frequency at which horses' minds vibrate. Horses are telepathic and so project pictures and emotions. This gave me the means to understand how I had received Nancy's pictures and feelings of grief. That day in the stable I had been practising reiki, getting my busy thoughts, judgements, and mental projections out of the way. Essentially, I had opened a clear channel to experience thoughts, pictures, and emotions from Nancy—the same reason I was able to hear Nancy say "thank you" when the reiki woman came to visit. My only regret is that I had freaked out and left the stable in a panic. Who knows what else I may have learned that day had I understood then what was really happening.

I put this knowledge to use from that day on even if I was unable to hear or see further insights from Nancy. I would regularly hold images in my head and focus on them whilst in the company of horses, my own and those I tended to at work. Walking the yearlings out in hand in preparation for the sales was usually a task that came with the potential for excitable and sometimes dangerous behaviour. One youngster would get excited and start leaping and rearing, which would set all the others off. Sometimes one would get away and go racing around the paddock and charging back towards the rest of us, setting all the others off. The potential for injury to the horses and to us was always present, so working on the premise that this communication through imagery could work both ways, I used to hold the image of a huge bowl of feed waiting in the stable for the yearling I was walking. I would keep counting in the four-beat walking rhythm and imagine all four feet staying on the ground, heading towards the bowl of feed. No matter what was kicking off around me, I just focused on this and kept walking. Invariably, the young horse I was holding just ignored the ruckus and carried on. I just trusted that if the image was in my mind, then the horse would pick it up.

One day at work, one of the more unpredictable colts had seemingly tried to jump out of his stable, literally through the door, which was now lying on the ground three feet away from the stable. He was limping about with blood everywhere from lacerations to his front legs. I had to hold onto him whilst Ellie tended to his injuries as we waited for the vet. Now this is tricky at the best of times with young horses, but this particular colt was so hormonal that he could lose all reason at any moment and become completely irrational and lethal with his legs. The seriousness of the situation and my desire not to get injured meant my focus was so intent (imagining his feet being glued to the floor) that I must have freed my mind of all other chatter. Not only did this give me something to occupy myself with and allowed me to feel that I was helping him in some way, but also it opened a channel for him to share with me what happens to him when he loses control, particularly around fillies. I encountered, albeit briefly, an immense black weight falling over me, and it was impossible to see, hear, or feel anything but a terrifying numb darkness. I felt that I needed to run and fight for my life and that I had no control over it all. My own heart was racing in my chest. I knew instantly that this was what happened to this young colt in those moments when he was seemingly out of control. I always knew that the hormonal response to the fillies would trigger it, along with any other experience that he perceived as frightening.

It was terrifying and all-consuming. In that moment, I understood how awful it was for him to feel this oppressive black veil coming down upon him and not be able to control it. Understanding it was his feelings, not mine, that I was experiencing, I was able not to freak out this time. I quietly sent back feelings of safety and calmness and imagined I was holding his hoof in support. I have no clue if it helped, but I did it all the same.

He had stood completely still that morning to have his legs cleaned and bandaged until the vet could get to him. And he was an absolute trouper throughout his recovery too. He was one of my yearlings to prep that year, so I was able to understand his behaviour from that day forward and try to help him as best I could by remaining calm myself and employing my imaging tactics to help him make sense of all the new experiences that he had to go through. Who knows if it helped him. But, if nothing else, I was developing my ability to control my thoughts and not get distracted (which I had discovered was a huge hurdle for me). I also learned that we as humans don't always understand what it's like in an animal's shoes; I would never have imagined the colt was going through these things until he showed me. I have fond memories of him. When he finally went off into training, I was sad to see him go. I was then thrilled to hear a few weeks later that he had been the bravest one who would lead all the other new ones out each morning and courageously lead them over and past new obstacles. *Good for him!* I thought.

# CHAPTER 5

# KINESIOLOGY

I continued to try, but I was never able to reach that place or frequency again with Nancy. I didn't realise at the time, but I would never quite master the art of calming my mind enough to see a repeat of this kind of transferred information because of so much turmoil in my private life and having massive time restrictions.

The second course I enrolled on was Touch for Health Kinesiology. I tell people that I had chosen this because the Chinese have understood energy and worked with energy healing for thousands of years and I wanted to know how to use this in such a way as to explore the possible areas of physical disease in Nancy's body. In reality, though, the only reason I chose to study kinesiology was because I had asked out loud to the universe or whoever, in desperation really, to give me a sign as to what to do next. I subsequently kept hearing the word *kinesiology* on the radio, hearing it in conversations, reading it in books, etc. I had been reading loads of books that I had been recommended on the animal communication course—some amazing books on all sorts of topics—and I was beginning to see how closed off my mind had been to so many things. It was kind of contagious; the more I read, the more I needed to know. There were fascinating animal-based memoirs, books about the human mind, books about animal totems, and some on other healing methods I'd never heard of, such as kinesiology. Having known nothing about kinesiology, I suddenly discovered that it seemed to be everywhere! I know it sounds mad, but I took that as a sign and enrolled on the next course. It seemed to be the way things were rolling in this quest to help Nancy, so off I went. I really had no idea what I was about to learn or how much it would help me understand things years down the line. It turned out to be the best foundation for everything else that followed on this journey of discovery. I still use elements of it every day.

Chinese medicine is such a massive topic that it would take a lifetime to understand it all, but suffice to say that John Thie, founder of Touch for Health (TFH) Kinesiology, had used some Chinese medicine theory and incorporated it into his modern healing practice in Australia. He developed a method of muscle testing and hands-on healing that anyone could learn in order to help themselves. He called it "touch for health". This was a really good place to start. Energy that flows through everything can get blocked. The idea of learning how to use muscles and muscle testing as a physical means to find the blockages and then release them sounded not only fascinating but also useful. Remember, at this point I still had no idea where the pain was in Nancy's body, so I had no means to help her heal. I was desperate to find something to give me a clue as to where her problem was.

First, I learned the forty-eight key muscles of the human body that are also energetically connected to the fourteen main meridians and organs of the body and how to effectively use muscle testing to detect anomalies in their integrated functions. I learned to understand the effect of light touch and how this can give feedback as to the condition of the body and can also affect a change in said body. Muscle testing highlights a conflict in the mind as well as in the physiological body, highlighting differences between conscious and subconscious beliefs. This was my first foray into the territory of mental well-being, the beginning of understanding that to change patterns of behaviour and to heal was something that needed to be done on a subconscious level, not just a conscious level. Muscle testing highlighted the conflicting truths of my conscious thoughts and my subconscious beliefs. I also had fun muscle testing with foods, colours, and chemicals. It clearly showed which of these were not beneficial to each of us at that time. Turns out tea was a no for me! Crazy, I thought, as I lived on tea and didn't think it was causing a problem for me. That was until I went wild camping for a weekend soon after and I forgot to take the teabags. I had to go for three days without tea. This left me with a monumental headache to start with, but I also realised that my back pain that always woke me in the night had gone. I had slept brilliantly in my tent each night. When I got home, I started drinking tea again, and sure enough my back pain started up and I couldn't sleep through it. I cut tea out of my diet and went through the monumental headache again. I have not drunk tea since. Funnily enough, I don't miss it. This did surprise me as I'd lived on tea since I was thirteen years old and would never have imagined a day without it.

The other fascinating thing I learned on the course is how trauma memory is held in the physical body. Trauma can be physical trauma or emotional trauma. We who were enrolled were taught a technique to help release this trauma memory. I was staying at my brother's house whilst on this course as he lived much closer than I did to the location. I would practise each evening, on him or his wife, whatever it was I had learned each day. They were great guinea pigs. We did have a laugh at all the things I had to do; some of the ideas behind TFH kinesiology were still a little out there for me at this stage, but I was quickly becoming converted to the unexplainable because the results were proof that change had happened. The most alarming proof, however, was when I had practised the technique of releasing trauma memory on my brother's wife one evening. All had gone well, and I felt that I understood the technique, so I had gone back to class the following day to report as much. I then got a phone call around midday from my brother, who was a little panicked, to say the least. His wife had been teaching a rider that morning in her outdoor school and had suddenly collapsed, winded and gasping for air, complaining of shoulder and chest pain. The pupil had dismounted, called for help, and then carried her into the house to wait for my brother. He was now on the phone to me, asking what the hell I had done to her the previous evening. He was not amused. Although I calmly told him what we had been working on, I was also panicking inside and just a little alarmed myself! So I said I'd ring him back in five minutes as I was going to talk to my mentor about it. My mentor told us not to panic (a little late for that, I thought!). Once she had been brought up to speed with what had happened, she gave her advice on what to do, and very quickly my brother's wife recovered.

The issue we had been working on the previous evening was to do with my sister-in-law's loss of confidence in jumping her horses. It was the act of leaving the ground that was causing her problems. Fixing this had been the goal during the trauma memory release technique. Her body had processed it and was letting go of the trauma memory from a crashing fall she had had out hunting several years earlier. During the fall, she had experienced being winded, breaking her collarbone and some ribs, and injuring her shoulder. She was now physically going through the crash again, feeling it all in her body (unfortunately not very pleasant for her). But in the end it freed her body of that memory. She began to jump her horses again not long after. The fascinating thing was that when my mentor told them what to do, to run the meridians involved in the trauma, my brother watched on as two physical lumps moved slowly down his wife's arm, following the line of the meridians and out of her hand. As they disappeared, she declared she felt great! He couldn't believe that he could actually see her body letting go of the trauma! Powerful but scary stuff! My mentor was pleased with my efforts, but I was just a little cautious to go practising again because this crazy shit could actually drop people to the floor!

I thoroughly enjoyed this course. It gave me a really good background to understand how energy works in the body and how to tap into it to get feedback. I had a great time learning all the muscles and meridians. My daughter would help me revise for my exams. We had coloured pictures and images of muscle groups stuck up all around the house to help me visualise them, and in the process she became a very adept muscle tester herself. It is a fabulous thing for her to have learned and to have as a basic understanding of her body—how the muscles, meridians, and organs are all connected and how she can affect them. I was also becoming more aware of my own state of mind, how my body was reacting to the emotional stress of my marriage and business, and what it needed to improve the situation. Take for example the day I learned how colour can heal certain emotions. For me at this time, it was emotions about my personal predicament that I had tried so hard to quash and hide from myself and from the world. The poor woman whom I'd been partnered with for the practice session had to deal with a tidal wave of anger and resentment, followed by uncontrollable laughter. The muscle testing indicated that the colour green was what I needed to focus on, or wear, or touch that day. It also revealed I needed to shout to get some healing of this situation, but I was so self-conscious that I could barely squeak. However, given an empty room, a green towel to hold and look at, and some time to myself, I soon found my shout—and then I couldn't stop shouting and ranting and stamping my foot like a spoilt kid! It's funny looking back, but I can now see that I was really in a mess emotionally—shut down and confused with no skills to deal with it. How could I have had those skills? This is not something that we are prepped for in school. I could sew a teddy bear, do mental arithmetic, read a book, and bake a cake, but deal with life and the shit it threw at me? Hell no! No skills for that. Kinesiology was giving me a tool to read my body and how it was coping with life—or not coping in my case. It was clear from all the muscle testing that I needed to have a really hard think about my situation and what I needed to change to improve my body's responses. I was in a lot of pain in my pelvis and lower back, and it had been slowly getting worse over the past couple of years. Although the chiropractor repeatedly worked on me to keep me mobile, it was getting worse and I didn't know what to do. Muscle testing was indicating emotional causes for this pain, which translated to *Stop burying your head in the sand about your marriage!* Scary? Yes. But no denying it when I could feel my muscles respond in such ways to indicate a real lack of homeostasis. There was disease in my body and mind, and I was heading towards serious problems if I were to continue to ignore it.

So here I was, faced with starting to admit I could see that I couldn't just stay as I was. Sticking my head in the sand about my marriage and hoping for some miraculous cure for how I felt just wasn't helping. But what to do about it? Financially and emotionally, I was in no position to leave my husband as I wasn't then able to support myself and my daughter. The situation was further complicated by the fact that I was also a foster carer, and a damn good one, and had children staying with us all the time. I didn't want to let them down either. I felt trapped now and very alone. So I put my head back in the sand for a while longer, leaned on Jacko for strength and support, and turned my attention once again to Nancy.

# CHAPTER 6

# MASTERSON METHOD

I had had my eyes opened to the world of energy and had an understanding of emptying my mind to become receptive to animal communication. I had experienced energy healing and muscle testing, but now I wished to learn a more physiological-based modality. Nancy's body, through muscle testing, had also revealed that she needed some muscular and deep tissue therapy.

In the first equine massage course I did, I learned techniques of massage and trigger point work. Although it was a great introduction to equine anatomy and function, I found that I was still unable to get a clear picture of what was troubling Nancy physiologically. She would stand nice and quiet whilst I practised my massage techniques, and she seemed to enjoy it for the most part, but I felt there was something I was always missing. I couldn't read her body; I couldn't get into the real Nancy at all. I guess this is why all those other therapists couldn't tell me anything useful after they had treated her. I felt the same, as if there was no feedback. I felt that I was just working on her outside shell and not reaching her inside. So, how do I reach her inside?

I sat in front of my computer searching equine massage/ bodywork most evenings, looking for the answer, and all that kept popping up was some American guy working on his horses. I wanted to find something here in the UK, so I just kept bypassing the annoying American, who seemed to be everywhere in my computer, hijacking every page I looked at. I kept scrolling through lots of papers and video clips of therapy work for horses. Nothing was getting my attention, and nothing was really answering the question, so as I was just about to shut off my computer one evening, feeling dejected, a video clip popped up of that bloody American guy again, but all I read was "bladder meridian". That sat me up straightaway. I watched as this American guy, Jim Masterson, ran his hand along the bladder meridian of a horse and explained his "Search, Response, Stay, Release" method to the viewers. I watched in awe as Jim searched with his hand along the bladder meridian of the horse (search), and when the horse blinked (response), he kept his hand where it was (stay). Then, just a short while later, the horse began licking and chewing and then yawning a lot (release). Lighting had just struck me as I realised this was the missing link, the answer I had been looking for, a means to get feedback and reach the inside of Nancy. I sat up all night watching everything that Jim Masterson (the *not* so annoying American guy now, funnily enough) had put up on his website or elsewhere on the internet, or anything else I could find. I learned he had four measures of pressure he used—air gap, egg yolk, grape, and lemon—and that mostly he was working in air gap and egg yolk (the pressure it would take to dent an egg yolk with your finger). Most importantly, if the horse was not responding or got agitated, he always went softer. *Softer*—not harder, but *softer!* Amazing! Light touch was something I was familiar with from kinesiology, so this made a great deal of sense to me. I ordered Jim Masterson's DVD and book *Beyond Horse Massage* straightaway and then enrolled on his weekend course that he was teaching here in the UK, in Cornwall, in just a fortnight's time. Boy oh boy, my husband was not going to be happy. But funny how the universe was helping me out big time. At least it was in the UK, not the USA! I was going to make it no matter what. I just knew I had to be there. No doubt in my mind that this was it. I couldn't sleep now, I was so excited. And I couldn't wait for the sun to come up so I could get to the stables and have a go at the bladder meridian with Nancy and Jacko.

The first bladder meridian with Nancy saw her falling into that lovely semi-sleepy trance-like state that I had witnessed when the reiki woman worked with her. Finally, I had achieved that relaxed demeanour; it had only taken me two years! Nancy blinked like crazy and licked and chewed like I'd never seen her do before. She pulled faces and twitched and did all manner of weird responses. Her head lowered so much that her nose was almost on the floor, and she was all wobbly on her feet. It was the most feedback I had ever seen from her in the three years she had been with me. To be honest, I would have been ecstatic with a lick and a chew, but this was off-the-scales amazing! I played around with how light my touch was, and sure enough, the lighter I was, the more responses I got. I also realised that she braced right up when I was on her neck on the right side, nowhere else. This was a massive clue as I had never had so much feedback before and still had no idea where her pain was or what the problem was. My goodness. I was so excited now that I couldn't wait to go on the course.

OMG! Finally, I was really there, at the Jim Masterson weekend clinic, sitting in the classroom, nervous as hell but excited to start learning. With all the turmoil at home, my self-confidence was at an all-time low. I was feeling like such a failure in life at this point that it was an absolute miracle I was even sitting there. Having argued, stood my ground, and convinced my husband I needed to do this, I had driven all the way to Cornwall and was now sitting in a room full of strangers. I was way out of my comfort zone. As I listened to everyone introduce themselves very eloquently, I was dreading my turn. So, as you can probably imagine, whilst blushing furiously, sweating, and fidgeting, I could barely make myself say my name, never mind explain why I was there, so I mumbled something about

Nancy and kinesiology and then shrank back into my chair. Great start, Helen!

Reminding myself I was there for Nancy, I tried as best I could to put my own uncomfortable situation aside and focus. The Masterson method was everything I hoped for and more, and Jim's entertaining character very quickly put me at ease. He was very funny and very clever. Boy, did I learn a lot that weekend. I met some other very wonderful people that weekend who have gone on to become good friends, but I would like to make a particular mention of the coaches as they were truly amazing that weekend. Guiding me and helping me to relax and understand the techniques, they took me under their wing. I'm forever grateful to them. Whether they knew it or not, I really needed my confidence to be boosted—and they did it. That weekend changed the way I worked with horses forever. Not only did I learn some great techniques for releasing muscular tension, and how horses show this release of tension, but also I learned about the natural brace response of a horse and how to work under it. As flight animals, horses are programmed to hide their weaknesses or problems for fear of being the next meal for a predator or being kicked out of the herd for being weak. When we as therapists put pressure on them, they use that pressure to brace against and hide their weakness. By staying under that brace response and giving them nothing to brace against, we can effect a release of muscular and mental tension by triggering their parasympathetic nervous system to relax. That is why the softer we are, the greater the release of tension. Less is more. It's wonderful. For those who are sceptical, the proof is in the behaviour of the horse. I had seen nothing like this, and I'd never seen so many horses all responding in the exact same way over the weekend, no matter the breed, age, or discipline.

Needless to say, I spent hours watching, reading, and practising on Jacko and Nancy. And every time I was blown away by their responses, I was getting to the inside of my horses, and the bond between us just rocketed. They looked at me differently, and I saw them differently now, but it felt so natural. I loved working *with* the horses in this way instead of working *on* the horses. It wasn't just my own horses either. As I mentioned earlier, I was working at a stud at this time, and the owner, Ellie, was really supportive as I was learning the Masterson method. She would encourage me to practise on her horses. She had to be quite persuasive too at times as my low self-image kept getting in my way and I'd find excuses not to practise. Operating a thoroughbred stud that also took in visiting racehorses for holidays or rehab, I was fortunate enough to get hands-on experience with a plethora of horses with different problems and of different ages. Ellie really believed in me and gave me the courage to take on a horse that had come to her in quite bad shape. Ginger Lucy we called her. She had been racing but had broken down, so she'd arrived at Ellie's for veterinary assessment and rehab. However, the prognosis wasn't great. Poor Ginger Lucy was very sore everywhere; she was lame and couldn't move well at all in any gait. The vet told the owner that it could take a month or more of intensive therapy work at his clinic to get this horse right—and even then it was a fifty-fifty chance that she wouldn't ever make it back to the racetrack. And it would cost rather a large sum of money to do the therapy on her. Well, this was not the news any of us were hoping for, but when the owner turned to me and said, "So, what about this bodywork you have been studying? Could you help her?" I nearly died of shock! He then followed that question with "I'll give you six weeks to work on her, and if she is no better by then, she will be shot." The vet agreed to let me work on her, so that was that. Ginger Lucy's life was now in my hands—literally! I couldn't believe what had just happened. If it hadn't been for the support and encouragement of Ellie and a dear friend, Beth, whom I worked with at the stud, I would never have learned the lesson I was about to learn.

Ginger Lucy was known to Ellie as she had stayed with her at the stud before, so Ellie knew she had broken her pelvis as a young filly. Therefore Ginger Lucy had always been a little wonky in her hind end. However, the way she was moving now saddened Ellie greatly as clearly this mare was in pain and very restricted in her range of motion in all limbs. We couldn't touch her anywhere without her flinching away in pain, and she was very switched off mentally. So where oh where was I to start?

At this point, I had done only the weekend course with Jim Masterson. Although I had my massage and kinesiology training too, I felt a little overwhelmed to say the least. So I decided that the best thing to do was to work with Ginger Lucy every third day and only for half an hour each time. This was all her nervous system could take really. She certainly was not able to withstand deeper massage work because she was so sore, so I practised only the Masterson method (MM) on her for six weeks. Of course the bladder meridian was the very first thing I did. Her response to that very light touch, as I ran the whole meridian, was extraordinary. I worked up to doing some of the other techniques when she was able to tolerate more. About three weeks in, during one session, she woke up. What I mean by this is that she had been very switched off mentally, and although her body was responding to the MM, up to this point she had still been operating like a robot mentally. But on this particular day, her eyes opened, really opened, and looked clear and alive. She coughed and snorted and shook and yawned like crazy—you know, those yawns where the eyeballs roll back up into the head? She was also throwing her head around gaily as she yawned. It was a wonderful moment. From then on, she stayed in the room with me mentally, looking at me, interacting with me, and being really inquisitive. I hadn't realised just how switched off she had been until she was actually present. She stayed present from that day on and continued to release tension, but in a more interactive way, pointing to her body where she needed help, nuzzling my hands, and positioning herself for the work. I loved it and looked forward to the days I worked with her so I could see her transform and relax.

Ginger Lucy lived in a lovely hay barn, so she could move about more freely than if she were in a stable, but she never came out of there during the six weeks. So when D-Day arrived and the vet came back to assess her, none of us knew how she would move on a firm surface or even if she could move! The vet, the owner, Ellie, and I watched on as Beth walked Ginger Lucy up and down the hard track and then took her into the lunge pen to trot her. I could hardly breathe and wanted to run and hide, but also I so wanted to see Ginger Lucy prove to everyone that she deserved a chance to live— don't forget her life was on the line here. It wasn't her fault she had ended up so sore and crippled. I was rooting for her wholeheartedly, as were Beth and Ellie, so I stayed and watched—albeit through my fingers!

Ginger Lucy blew us all away; she moved around the lunge pen with a powerful, free movement and looked absolutely amazing! No lameness, no hesitation, and no difference between left and right rein. It was easy for her, and beautiful to watch. She was enjoying it as much as we were. All our mouths were open in disbelief. I heard Ellie say, "She has never moved like that before, ever." The vet asked me what the hell I was training in, so I told him about Jim Masterson and the Masterson method. He simply said, "Well, please carry on, as that is an unbelievable transformation. Well done, Helen." Ginger Lucy lived! She lived to race again.

The lesson I learned from that six weeks with Ginger Lucy was that even with just the basic techniques of the Masterson method, following the horse's responses with light touch only, staying under the brace response, I was able to release that horse's full range of motion. I was able to help the whole body and mind of the horse to relax, thereby allowing her to make the changes necessary deep within herself. How powerful a lesson that was. I have never forgotten it. Even if the weekend course were all I ever did and the basic techniques were all I ever learned from Jim Masterson, I was able to save a horse's life with it! Bloody awesome! Of course, I went on to do the five-day course, followed by the fieldwork course and the three-day certification course to become a fully qualified Masterson method practitioner and then coach. How could I not after that? Today I love every minute I spend in the company of horses, searching for their responses and waiting for the releases, helping them back to their full potential. A huge *thank you* to Jim Masterson for being that annoying American who seemed to invade my computer all those years ago!

Learning about the natural brace response of the horse, I began to understand why Nancy could stand there whilst I and other therapists worked *on* her. The harder we worked on her, the more she had to brace against, so she could easily block us out. When I first began Masterson method work *with* Nancy, her eyes popped out her head. She looked very startled that I was giving her nothing to brace against and her nervous system had to respond. She really wasn't sure how to deal with it and became fidgety and evasive, trying to distract herself, and me, from what I was doing. Now the human response to this would normally involve more force, but I had learned to go softer, so she felt a change from me. For her to feel this change and to know I had listened to her and understood her discomfort but had not stopped helped her to release the tension. This was the only way to progress, allowing the nervous system to respond and help her relax. She did relax eventually, but it took months of patience and practice before I really felt that I was beginning to unravel the puzzle that was Nancy. Don't forget that I was learning too and would regularly make the human error of trying too hard, asking for too much, and not being light enough. Nancy was a superb teacher, initially frustrating as hell, to be honest, but I learned so much from those early attempts that the learning was quick. I did then start to see changes in her. I also found out where she was absolutely not allowing me to go and where she was happy for me to go. Over the next twelve months, I unravelled Nancy little by little, until I was left with two areas of restriction where she had a limit as to what she could cope with. This led me finally to understand, with the help of my new vet (the same brilliant vet who had come to the stud), that she had received an injury to her neck as a youngster which had affected the nerves all down the right side of her body. To be ridden was very painful for her. And although that wonderful, stoic little mare had always tried her hardest to allow humans to ride her, it was never going to get better for her. Therefore, I decided that she would never be ridden again. My main concern now was to make sure she remained as comfortable as possible at all times and to find her a little job.

# CHAPTER 7

# MOTHERHOOD

Nancy was a nicely bred thoroughbred with a really gentle character and great conformation, so it seemed to me there was one "job" that she really deserved the chance at: to be a mum again! Having worked for years at the stud and having watched as the mares' character and traits always came through in the youngsters, I knew Nancy had the perfect attributes for motherhood. Her problem was from injury, not from hereditary problems. We also knew now, from my adventures into the world of animal communication, that she had already had a foal, so she wasn't a maiden. My daughter and I discussed this at length. If we were going to do this, then there was no way we could ever sell the foal, for our own sentimental reasons, but also we couldn't do that to Nancy. She would have the say as to when it was weaned, and they would always be kept together for as long as we had them both. I consulted the vet to make sure pregnancy wouldn't in any way cause a problem with her neck and nerves, and he agreed it was a great idea.

So the excitement of finding the stallion began. My daughter and I both wanted a native stallion, so we shortlisted a few breeds and finally decided on a Connemara. To be honest, I think we both knew this was inevitable as Jacko meant the world to us both and he was an Irish sports pony (thoroughbred × Connie). He was intelligent, athletic, fun, and safe. There could never be too many Jackos in the world. So began the very tricky and complicated process of choosing the right Connemara stallion. This entailed printing off photos of the shortlisted ones and taking them to Nancy, who then kept placing her nose on the same photo no matter how many times we mixed them up. That was that! So, very *not* tricky or complicated! Nancy chose Charlie. So off to Wales we went to meet the lovely Kingstown Charlie.

Anyone who has bred their own horses will know that we all have our own preferences for what we look for in a stallion. I wasn't particularly interested in any ridden achievements. In fact, my only two criteria were as follows:

1. The horse would have a genuinely nice personality and be gentle and kind.
2. He would have good conformation and bone with no hereditary physical conditions.

I had seen mares and stallions pass on twisted legs with poor conformation, leading to expensive intervention to correct it. I had handled youngsters that, even though they were treated the same as all the other young horses, had still been very difficult and quirky to work with (just like the stallion people would say). I recall one mare always used to have foals that were born head-shy, just like her. Up until then, I had believed head-shyness came from poor handling by humans or an injury to the head.

Charlie was wonderful. He met both my criteria on the day we went to see him. His owner was lame herself, and although she happily caught Charlie and walked him about, she was clearly struggling and slower than normal. Charlie was a perfect gentleman and didn't once pull, or barge, or cause her any grief at all; he stood quietly and moved when asked. He was just a gentle soul with a kind eye. There were mares all around and youngsters running about, but he just quietly and politely did what his owner asked, no fuss. He was 15 hands high, which is quite big for a Connemara, but that was fine with me as Nancy was 15.2 hands high, so there was every chance, hopefully, we would get a foal that would grow to a similar size. Perfect for us (we are not blessed with lovely long legs!). Ellie had taught me well. My years of looking at horses and assessing their conformation came in handy now. As I cast my eye over Charlie and smiled, every box was ticked. My daughter and I drove home smiling. Nancy had chosen Charlie from photos (which a lot of people thought was a crazy way to go about choosing a stallion), and now after we'd met him and spent time with him, we knew he was perfect. Nancy had clearly chosen well. We had no need to look at other stallions, so that was that. The arrangements were made for Nancy to go and visit Charlie.

# CHAPTER 8

# THE POWER OF EQUINE HEALING

━━━━━⌇━━━━━

It was around this time that I was beginning to understand Jacko's role in my life better. Although I had acknowledged early on his role as my rock and support, I was also witnessing another phenomenon about him. Our time together gave me a front-row seat to witness the gentle but powerful healing that Jacko facilitated with the young kids from troubled backgrounds. Although he was jolly, excitable, and generally a bouncing bubble of energy to ride, he was also the gentlest and safest horse to handle and be around. The kids loved him, and he was a tonic for many a child. They would migrate to his stable, and this gentle soul would help them to think and talk. It was always in his stable that they disclosed traumas that otherwise they struggled to voice. They would comment on how he made them feel calm and safe. I sat for many an hour in his stable on upturned buckets with various kids, whilst Jacko munched his hay, and they opened up and began to heal. It was as if he cocooned them in an invisible safety net, hugging them with his calming energy, and they felt it. They trusted that he would catch them when they let their defences fall away. It is heartbreaking to hear and see a child fall apart as he or she talks about things that have hurt and terrified him or her. It is magical, however, to witness a wonderful horse like Jacko hold the space for these kids to begin to heal. One little boy who came to stay would awake in the night and ask me if it was a good time to go and see Jacko. I would reply, "It's always a good time to go and see Jacko." So, no matter the time or weather, off we would go, and Jacko, sometimes as bleary-eyed as I, was always gracious and tolerant of us invading his stable. Sometimes the kids would lean against Jacko; sometimes they would just have a hand on his leg or neck; and sometimes they would just be sitting in the corner of the stable or playing with Jacko's tail. Jacko would just munch his hay and look as relaxed as ever, but he wouldn't move a muscle until they were done talking. I can't tell you how much he helped these kids. I was in awe at the capacity of his understanding of it all! Healing was his thing, and time and time again he demonstrated that he knew just what to do to help.

One day Jacko had to stand still for over an hour whilst I built a large platform around him. The predicament we found ourselves in was a little unusual, to say the least. I had staying with me a teenage girl who loved the horses and had asked if she could ride. I had tacked Jacko up and had led him around the village and lanes whilst she sat on board, grinning like a Cheshire cat the whole time. As always, Jacko had been a perfect gentleman and had been jolly enough to make us laugh without being scary or dangerous. He always judged his pilots perfectly and knew just how much enthusiasm to put into his job! We arrived back at the stables, and that's when we became aware of the monumental problem we had. The teenager had a condition called cerebral palsy, and she coped admirably with everything she did. However, what we hadn't figured was that whilst she was able to mount a horse quite well with help and sit comfortably, her muscles would relax and lengthen whilst riding, so now she couldn't work her legs normally to dismount!

She was stuck fast on top of Jacko. No matter how much we tried, every which way we could think of, we just couldn't get her off Jacko. It was also just her and me; there was no one else around to help. I kept a smile plastered firmly in place so as not to belie the panic that was building underneath, but I was absolutely perplexed as to how to get her off. Thank goodness it was Jacko she was on. He just stood perfectly still and waited. Not fidgeting, not getting upset, he just waited quietly. I finally decided that I was going to have to build a platform high enough to stand above the girl and literally lift her off with brute strength. Luckily, we had a collection of pallets, hay bales, and the forever useful baler twine! What would we do without baler twine? So, as you can imagine, this took me quite awhile to construct, making it big enough and safe enough to perform the extraction. Jacko was still standing perfectly still whilst all this was going on around him. Eventually, the moment of truth came. I clambered up on top of this now epic mounting block and prayed that I could find the strength to lift the girl off. It didn't go quite as smoothly as I had envisioned in my mind, but I did finally manage to get her off Jacko and onto the platform (panic and adrenalin mostly). The next problem was that she couldn't use her legs at all now; they had gone to sleep! Jacko had to stay where he was for another ten minutes or so whilst we massaged her legs and got the feeling back into them to enable her to climb down off the platform. Only then was I able to thank that wonderful horse for being so amazing and get him out of the epic build and back to his field. All I could think was, *Now I know what those hoists that I have seen in the posh arenas are for!*

# CHAPTER 9

# POISONED

It was through Jacko that I was introduced to the power of homeopathic medicine. When Jacko was twenty years young, he had an unfortunate incident with a new, young tractor driver on the farm. In his naivety, this young man had driven into Jacko's field and sprayed fertiliser whilst he was in there. Not only did Jacko ingest some, but also he had galloped about (understandably) whilst the sprayer was in his field—and that particular year, the dry spring ground was hard as concrete. The outcome of this was concussive and toxic laminitis. Laminitis is a debilitating inflammation and subsequent breakdown of the soft tissue in the hoof (called the laminae) that holds the bones of the foot in place within the hoof wall. There are many causes, but all cases have the same outcome. Most cases can be caught quickly enough and reversed with the horse recovering after a few weeks with no lasting ill effects. However, if not diagnosed quickly enough and the horse is allowed to continue to move about, then it can quickly escalate to the soft tissue dying and the bones of the hoof falling through the sole of the foot. In Jacko's case, it was a toxic reaction to the fertiliser, coupled with the concussive galloping on the hard ground, that had caused his laminitis. On top of this, the vet I used at the time misdiagnosed it twice. First the vet thought Jacko had "tied up"—a painful condition caused by trauma to the muscle tissue which can lead to a rise in the dying muscle cells, releasing enough toxic debris into the bloodstream to stress the kidneys. Then she changed her mind and forced me to walk him for hours in hand—the worst thing to do for acute laminitis. For two days, the vet tried to tell me that it was colic and that Jacko quite possibly had a twisted gut. "At his age, surgery is risky, so you should put him to sleep," she said. OMG, I couldn't believe this was happening, not to Jacko, dearest Jacko. I looked at him. He looked at me. His expression was clearly one of, *Do not let that woman near me.* I told her clearly then and there that there was another option: she was going to leave, and I was going to get a second opinion. That is exactly what I did. And I asked the wonderful vet whom Ellie had used at the stud to come and see Jacko. He had been the stud vet for years, and I had seen him in action many times. I watched with relief as he came out very quickly and began his diagnosis. He wasted no time and quickly concluded we should treat Jacko for laminitis, *not* untreatable colic! However, the relief didn't last long. The enforced walking the first vet had insisted on had done its damage. Over the next twelve months, Jacko went through hell and back. Three of his pedal bones (foot bones) rotated and nearly pushed through his soles, and the pockets of gas and pus that accumulated in his feet were relentless. The new vet's care and knowledge was second to none as he trimmed away Jacko's feet to varying degrees to free the necrotic tissue without permanently damaging them. Jacko was on high dosages of pain relief, and I was constantly bathing and cleaning his body and feet. If you have ever witnessed laminitis at its worst, you will know how hard it is to watch a horse endure the agony of the healing process. The afflicted horse literally has to grow new feet. Such horses cannot get up or move easily, so they lie down a lot, increasing the potential for large sores to develop on their sides and elbows. They need hand feeding regularly as they can't get to their food or water, and their muscles turn to concrete through lack of movement and a build-up of tension caused by the effort of compensating. Horses with laminitis distort themselves into bizarre shapes when they do stand in an effort to get off their painful feet, in Jacko's case, three of his feet! Jacko's body was also trying to detox. The vet told me that he usually got only one or two cases a year that were this bad, and not many horses were tough enough to get through it. Jacko was fighting his corner, though, so I would fight with him. This amazing horse seemed to know what was needed, to the point where he would hold a foot out, whilst still lying down, for the vet to trim it. When we needed to X-ray his feet, this being the most excruciatingly painful thing for us to ask Jacko to do, he would almost close his eyes, take a deep breath, lift his foot onto the wooden block, and hold it there. Understand that this meant he had to put all his weight onto the other feet that had also suffered pedal bone rotations—unbelievably painful even with pain relief. I have never witnessed such an act of true grit and stoicism from another horse, and I hope I never have to again. He was truly extraordinary.

Jacko was so poorly at one stage that I slept in his stable with him for ten nights, to be able to feed him and water him and tend to his needs. It was like an intensive care unit with the patient drugged up and out of it most the time. Except this nurse was not dressed accordingly the first night I slept in the stable. It happened to be my best friend's wedding night, but I had been called back home in the early hours by the woman who was looking after Jacko whilst I went to the wedding. She was very worried about him, so I left the wedding in all my finery and drove straight to the stable. I didn't leave him all night. In between caring for Jacko, I dozed on and off, wrapped in horse rugs, still wearing my bright green maxi dress, sandals, fascinator, and jewels! When the vet arrived in the morning, with straw in my fancy hairdo and make-up all smudged down my cheeks, I just got on with what we needed to do to get Jacko more comfy. I didn't give a thought to the picture I must have made! As he was leaving, the vet just smiled at me, shook his head, and said, "Go home, Helen. Jacko will be fine for a few hours." It was then that it dawned on me that I must have looked awful and maybe a little crazed! Tentatively looking in the car wing mirror, I was horrified at the member of the Addams Family crossed with Worzel Gummidge looking back at me!

On the tenth night, I must have dozed off, snuggled in the straw with a horse rug wrapped around me and much more appropriately dressed. I awoke abruptly to the sense of being watched! I slowly opened my eyes to find Jacko sitting up and looking at me with the most quizzical look on his face, as if saying, *What are you doing here?* He was clearly surprised to see me. I just smiled and said, "I am here for you." That was the moment I knew he would pull through; he was back in the room and fully present. I did everything I could for this stoic, incredibly tough horse. Amongst other things, I scoured the hedgerows for seasonal herbs and plants and offered them to him so he could self-select what he needed to heal (a strategy now known as zoopharmacognosy). He was on copious amounts of aloe vera, and my daughter and I muscle-balanced him (i.e. practised kinesiology) every week to ensure his meridians were clear and his organs were working to their optimum. To muscle test a horse, first you need a surrogate human who has been muscle tested and balanced, which in theory turns the person into a blank canvas. My daughter and I took it in turns to be the surrogate. Then, by placing a hand on Jacko and maintaining the contact throughout a second muscle test, conducted on whichever one of us was being the surrogate, the results/imbalances would be from Jacko's body, not ours. This gave us a clear picture of what he needed and when; sometimes he needed herbs, sometimes he needed more work by the vet, and sometimes he needed energy or lymphatic balance work. Even the vet commented one day that Jacko did not look as poorly as he actually was. His coat was shining, his eyes were bright, and because I washed and bathed him every few hours, he never had developed the sores and raw patches on his body and legs.

Ellie and Beth were both very supportive, Beth helping as much as she could with looking after him, Ellie allowing me to be rushing backwards and forwards from work to the yard (really disruptive to her business) and always offering great advice and support. As he got better, I was allowed to begin some gentle bodywork on him, but my oh my, where to start? His lumbar and hind end muscles where like concrete, and his shoulders were so tight that he could lose balance very easily. It was a matter of chipping away, little and often, giving his body time to adjust without overloading his lymphatic system with too many toxins. I also knew he would have to redevelop his proprioception when finally he went back out because of the months spent on a flat, soft surface. Proprioception is the sense of self-movement and/or body position and the ability to adapt to surroundings, particularly, in Jacko's case, the undulating ground beneath his feet. Mechanosensory (movement) neurons called proprioceptors, located within muscles, tendons, and joints, facilitate proprioception but need triggering all the time to maintain them. Jacko had been in his stable on a soft, flat surface for nearly a year and had therefore lost some of his proprioception. I needed to loosen up as much muscle as I could and give him his full range of motion back before he went out so as to help him to redevelop his proprioception and make a full recovery.

Eleven months later, Jacko was finally allowed out into a small woodchip paddock. I had been amazed at his tolerance at being in for so long. Such a bundle of energy was never easy to contain for long, and although initially he couldn't move much, as he began to recover I expected him to rebel a little or at least try to escape. However, he remained very calm and settled with his lot. The weather was beautiful, and I was toying with the idea of asking the vet if maybe it was time to get him out, when that afternoon I got to his stable and Jacko was rearing up at the door. I just smiled and laughed, saying, "OK, I get it. You are ready." He was making it clear that, yes, it was time; he was ready to go out. I rang the vet, and he agreed that I could put him in our woodchip paddock to see how he coped. What a wonderful moment. Jacko and I slowly and carefully made our way out across the hard driveway, through the top field, and across to the woodchip paddock gate. It was fabulous to have him outside again. The other horses all came over to be a part of it. Jacko, however, ignored them all and, completely out of character for him, pulled away from me before we got through the woodchip paddock gate and continued hobbling down the top field. He then broke straight through the electric fence into the bottom field, all at a steady but determined stiff walk, clearly on a mission. He never broke fences. Even if a fence were to come down in the wind, he would always be the one that stayed in his paddock. I had no idea where he was going, but I followed him right to the far corner of the bottom field, through two more electric fences, and into an overgrown, bramble-filled corner. He finally stopped and began to eat something as if his life depended on it. As I scrambled after him to see what it was he was now munching on, to my horror I discovered that he had eaten a whole large belladonna plant, otherwise known as deadly nightshade. *OMG, that's it!* I thought. *He is clearly committing suicide. All along he just wanted to die, and now he is taking steps to ensure this happens!* I was horrified and was only able to move him away from it once he had eaten the whole bloody plant. I was already on the phone to the vet as Jacko and I hobbled all the way back up to the woodchip paddock. But how did he know that plant was there? What was in that plant that he so desperately needed? I couldn't believe what had just happened. Of all the plants to eat, especially considering I had been foraging for months to bring him a massive selection of nonpoisonous plants to choose from, he had chosen this one.

Intrigued as I was, I spoke to a woman I had recently met who happened to be a homeopathic practitioner. She explained how homeopathic remedies work on the premise of treating like with like, so, for instance, Jacko had been poisoned and was treating himself with a poison, albeit a lower quantity/toxicity, that could help him heal quicker.

She also explained that ailments that yield to homeopathic belladonna are characterised by severe throbbing pains and can swiftly move to suppuration. This straightaway rang true for laminitis. So Jacko *was* self-healing, *not* trying to end it all! Remarkable, really, as there was no way I would have picked that plant and offered it to him as I did all the other plants. Clearly he knew he needed something in that plant, and he knew where to find it. As it was, Jacko spent the next two days looking as if he was high on something, completely spaced out but very, very happy!

What I learned throughout his incarceration was how healing is absolutely a whole mind and body process. It wasn't just about the wonderful practical scientific veterinary care; it was also about helping him stay mentally comfortable too. His physiological and energetic systems remained in optimum working order through kinesiology and the properties of certain plants that promote healing. But giving Jacko the opportunity to self-select and choose what he needed at different stages of the healing process was paramount to his mental health too. He was never on his own; he was given every opportunity to express his needs, and I listened. I even got to learn about the wonderful world of homeopathy, although in an alarming kind of way!

On a personal level, my introduction to the miracle healing power of homeopathy came when, some months later, something was making me ill—very ill. I had gotten to the point where it would take me four hours to get out of bed, get dressed, get in the car, and drive three miles to the stables. Ridiculous, I know, but everything was such an effort, as if my muscles just wouldn't or couldn't work. It took enormous willpower to move at all. I sat in the car trying really hard to summon the energy to open the door and get out. This had been going on for about a month and was gradually getting worse, but today was bad, really bad. I had also endured muscle spasms, a feeling of coldness all the time, uncontrollable shaking, hideous headaches, and nausea over the past few weeks. I was also aware that my temper had been very short and that I had been irrational of late.

So as I sat there feeling useless and pathetic, I literally shouted out in my frustration, "What the fuck is wrong with me?" And then I heard, as clearly as if someone was sitting next to me and speaking, "The car is killing you." I don't know whom or where it came from, but I was stunned. I like to think it was one of the horses, but I really don't know whom this voice belonged to. I owe whomever it was a big thank you, however.

I had bought the car I was sitting in a month prior. And yes, now that I thought about it, that was when all this started. It happened slowly, though, gradually worsening like creeping death, steadily getting worse rather than being sudden onset, so I hadn't really connected it. But, *yes*, the car was killing me! I thought back over the last month, which had been freezing cold, so I had had the heater on. Even when I was waiting to collect my daughter from school or a club, I left the car running to try to keep warm (something I wouldn't normally do). My daughter had twice fallen into an uncharacteristically deep sleep on the only two long journeys she had taken in the car with me—which now, I could see, was really weird and very worrying!

I rang the garage immediately and told them that I needed them to check my car over and explained why. I think they thought I was bonkers, but I was quite hysterical at this point, so they agreed to do it straightaway. To my relief, they found that the manifold was so loose that the fumes from the engine compartment were being sucked into the cab of the car. This particular model of car had the battery seated across the bulkhead, which allowed engine gases to enter the cab air intake! The mechanics thought the engine had been disconnected from the manifold to repair an oil leak at some point but had never been tightened back up. I had been driving around for a month inhaling toxic fumes and slowly being poisoned. The doctors said that of the list of symptoms for this type of poisoning, I had all but the last three—convulsions, unconsciousness, and death! The poison attaches itself to red blood cells, limiting the oxygen distribution around the body, hence why I was getting slower and slower, why everything was extremely hard work, and why I felt as if my brain was in a fog. The Doctor's said they had nothing they could give me to help with recovery. As long as the source of the poison had been removed, it was just time for my body to rid itself of the poison, which I was told might take a few days. So I waited and waited. After ten days I was no better, but no worse thankfully either! I still couldn't just get up, get dressed, and walk downstairs without having to stop and rest every few seconds. I couldn't work, or drive, or even walk the dogs, let alone muck out stables and ride. I didn't know what to do, so I turned to homeopathy for help.

I was lucky enough to have met Sara K when she asked me to work with her horse a few months earlier. He was a gorgeous black and white Cob that Sara K and her daughter had rehomed from the Blue Cross charity. As I was working with him, freeing his body of tension, Sara K was holding his halter. Suddenly she began to cry, and then I felt a surge of powerful energy come racing through his body and straight into my hands, which were resting on his hindquarters at the time. Whoosh! It was like nothing I had ever felt before. And then I was crying too! I looked at Sara K, she looked at me, and we both laughed out loud with tears running down our faces. She simply said, "Sorry about that. He needed ignatia for his sorrow." She then went on to explain she was an energy healer, having worked with a shamanic healer years ago, and was also a homeopathic practitioner. Wow, Sara K is a powerful healer. Over the years she has enlightened me to all sorts of healing modalities. On this occasion, however, she was about to introduce me to the true power of homeopathy. I would feel it for myself and feel the changes as they happened. She spoke with me at length, asking me loads of questions about myself and about the poisoning. She then gave me two small packets of pilules with instructions on when to take them. Now, although I was open to trying new things, particularly after all I had learned with Nancy and Jacko, I wasn't in a particularly positive frame of mind. My mind definitely wasn't clear yet, so I wasn't holding out much hope of these little pilules doing much for me. However, I followed the instructions and took these few remedies as instructed. After a day, I was up and about, feeling so much more in the room, not so spaced out, with more energy but still very slow and weak. Day 2 saw me up and about, feeling quite fine with my usual energy and ability to carry out any chores quickly and easily. I mucked out my stables, walked the dogs, and cleaned the house from top to bottom. Day 3 saw me back at work, feeling absolutely normal. Bearing in mind I worked at the stud, which meant heavy manual work and lots of walking, this was incredible. My head was clear, I felt happy and cheerful, and it almost felt as if the poisoning and symptoms had happened to someone else. Very quickly, almost too quickly to believe, I felt really good and not at all weak or useless. It was the quickest recovery but the weirdest recovery because it was so quick. It was absolutely amazing. I was so thankful to Sara K. For me, that was all I needed to know that from now on, homeopathy would be my first port of call whenever I needed a helping healing hand. It was extraordinary and wonderful. I have used homeopathy for many an ailment over the years since with equally swift and absolute results. This wonderful woman and I have become very good friends over the years. I thank my lucky stars that I had the opportunity to meet her and experience the wonderful healing of homeopathy. Jacko was right to show me. Through his and my recoveries, I now understand how all these many different healing modalities work together to help the body heal. There are so many times that a combination of homeopathy, kinesiology, and bodywork has restored and allowed for changes to take place that I no longer think it weird or different. It's just right to use everything at our disposal to help our bodies make the changes necessary to navigate back to homeostasis.

## CHAPTER 10

# BIRTHDAY

—◦◦◦—

So the big day had arrived. My daughter had her first ever race, rowing on Eton Dorney Lake. She had joined a local boat club and was a natural rower. She loved it—and today was race day. This meant an early start and lots to organise. However, Nancy was so close to foaling that I had been getting up to check her every few hours, so I was running late this morning, an hour late to be honest. What with packing and trying to remember everything for the race and sorting the young boys who were staying with us at the time, it was an unusually early start for them. I was tired, and now I was late. I was supposed to be with Nancy an hour ago, but it was now 5 a.m. As I drove into the yard and rushed to her stable, I found her backed up against the wall with her back legs crossed. As I opened the door, she sighed heavily, stepped forward, and began to give birth. I swear, she must have been waiting for me—and I was late, poor thing. It looked as if she had backed up to the wall to prevent the foal from coming out! Nancy just got straight down to business. Before I knew it, the legs and nose were right there. I barely had time to phone home and ask my husband to bring our daughter over to see this wonderful moment. She would never have forgiven me if I hadn't tried. As it was, they arrived just as Nancy gave birth to Nadur. We all watched in wonder as Nancy, who had clearly read the book on how to give birth perfectly, lay in the deep straw bed licking her foal clean. This wet little being was jet black with a white blaze down his face and a bright pink tongue sticking out. We all stood around Nancy, watching with delight as she licked him dry and eventually got up to help him suckle. It didn't take this smart little guy long to find the teat either. We all laughed when he emerged from under her with milk all over his nose! It was a magical moment, one that I will never forget. It also meant I had to think quick and reorganise the day. My husband took my daughter to her race. I took care of the new arrival and joined them later, just in time to see her race for the first time on the Olympic lake.

For months we had been thinking of names, and although we hadn't agreed on a girl's name, had it been a filly, we had semiagreed on the boy's name. Nancy was Nomadic Nancy, whose sire was Nomadic Way, so to continue the Nomadic theme and to honour our more natural ways of being with our horses, we decided Nomadic Nature would be a nice name. As the foal is half Irish (Connemara), we opted for the Gaelic translation of *nature*—Nadur. This is what I called him from that moment on. However, although my daughter liked the name, she thought that Flapjack was a much better name, so she has always called him that and still does!

Nancy was a natural and wonderful mother. She was in her element and had been so good to allow us to be a part of this magical moment, right in the stable with her every step of the way. We stayed for as long as we could and laughed as Nadur, unsteady on his feet and with milk all over his face, came straight over to us to investigate. He was not at all shy or worried—so very confident and intrigued right from the start. As I sat on a bale watching Nancy and feeling so happy for her that she now had the chance to be the mother she so desperately wanted to be, I also realised that this felt like the end of a journey and the beginning of a new one. I felt that the focus now had shifted from Nancy to Nadur, maybe. But then, as if struck with a bolt of lightning, I knew it had shifted from her to me!

# CHAPTER 11

# I DIDN'T KNOW I NEEDED HEALING

––––––⌒––––––

Nancy seemed blissfully happy about being a mum, but I continued with her bodywork just to ensure she stayed comfortable. I know now that our journey was never about me healing Nancy but about Nancy healing me. I was desperately unhappy when she came into my life. Through her and all the things I had learned to help her, I had been able to change and grow myself and start to really see where I was in my life at that moment.

I had travelled the world in my late teens and early twenties, had graduated from college, had been happily married for around ten years, had a wonderful, happy, healthy daughter, and had run our family business in local food retail and production with my husband. I had had no doubt in my mind when I married that it was for life, so I threw myself into it wholeheartedly. I thought my husband and I were very happy. And we worked hard to make a home and start a family.

For years, from the outside looking in, we appeared as a perfectly happy, normal, functioning family. On the inside, however, I could now admit that I didn't quite feel that. There was always this nagging feeling of not quite belonging, of something not being quite right, and the harder I tried to control things, the worse it got. There wasn't an exact moment when I began to realise all was not rosy in my world; it was more a steady sequence of events that had me questioning things and that left me baffled at the time. I recall, for example, when my husband would put staff members' needs before the family's, making me angry and causing me to feel that we were not as important. Looking back, I see there were lots of things I should have taken notice of but instead chose to ignore. One that should have made me really sit up and take note, however, was our moving house just two weeks after our daughter was born. This was before my husband and I had started the family business. This particular house came as a tied house to the job my husband had. The minute I walked into that house, I knew it was occupied with something other than spiders and humans. It was not at all welcoming. I had a flashback immediately to a house I had lived in when I was just six years old, a house I had tried to forget.

My family had moved from South Wales to Shropshire, and our temporary home, whilst my parents were looking to buy a house, turned out to be a house none of us will ever forget. The house that looked every bit the idyllic English country house with a circular sweeping driveway, bordered with masses of golden daffodils, took my breath away the minute we drove up to it. It was built in a semicircular shape, which as a six-year-old I thought was magical. As my siblings and I eagerly jumped out of the car to investigate, something stopped us abruptly. I remember just looking at the big old windows and knowing that we were being watched and not at all welcome. I really thought someone else still lived there, so I couldn't just run in. I waited for our mum and dad to take us in. As we entered, the feeling was horrible. For the next six months, I lived in fear. It was a terrifying house. As a young child who didn't really understand what was going on or why I felt so afraid, I never discussed it until months after we moved out. I now know that I am sensitive to energy, and that's why I felt so threatened. Being a sensitive means I sense energies/entities. I don't hear them or see them, but my body senses them. I also remember doors and cupboard doors flying open, lights going on and off all the time, and horrible noises amidst the sensation of being watched. Lots of accidents happened there, and the dog used to go mad at things we couldn't see. Just writing about this makes me shiver and causes the hairs on my arms to stand up.

It turns out I haven't yet forgotten that feeling. As I now walked into our new home twenty years later, I knew instantly as I was hit by a wave of menace that the house was not empty. Again I had to endure being touched on the shoulder by nothing, and being watched by nothing, and the dogs acting very protective of me and my baby daughter, watching and growling at things I couldn't see! I was a new mum and therefore was preoccupied with navigating this new role in life, but I think it was moving into this house that began to open my eyes to the fact that I felt lonely and was not listened to much of the time. It was the start of my realising that although I had thought I was happily married, I was seeing that I may have been wearing my rose-tinted glasses. I did not want to move into that house. I discussed this with my husband at length, but he ignored me. His thirst for advancement in his work overrode any "irrational" and "overemotional" wobbles I may have been experiencing. In fact, we moved into that house so fast that not even the water supply was connected or the kitchen fitted. How was I supposed to cater for a new baby with no water? My husband didn't seem to think this was a problem and was too excited to get out there to his new job. Luckily, my wonderful parents came to the rescue. Whilst Mum helped me with the baby, Dad plumbed in the water and fitted the kitchen— and they didn't leave until it was working. At the time, with my baby brain in full swing, I didn't think I had a choice. I know differently now, of course, but back then I was trying to do the right thing by my family, so I allowed myself to be ignored. When that job ended a year later, I was thrilled to be moving and kept telling myself that this would be a new start. I set up the new family business, looked after my daughter, and kept house (not haunted this time, thankfully). When the business was thriving a few years later and my husband joined it, that's when I began to see that nothing had really changed. He wasn't interested in my point of view, or my opinion on business decisions. I guess for many years it had been like this, but I had not wanted to see it. As the rose tint cleared, I began to see a lot of things differently. Holidays were a nightmare because even when a date had been set and arrangements made, he would declare last-minute "problems" had arisen at work to postpone, delay, or cancel them. If we did go, it was like it was my daughter and me on one agenda and my husband on another. I actually began to feel that we were not worth the bother to him as he was always preoccupied on the phone or needing to be somewhere else. I eventually put my foot down and went away anyway, with just my daughter, and began to notice how relaxed and happy we were when we did that. I began to tire of this facade that my husband lived behind and presented. To the outside world, including close family, we were perfectly happy. In reality, we were always pulling in opposite directions with opposite agendas of importance. I remember feeling very awkward when we did attend functions and parties as if I were just lying all the time to everyone around us, putting on a show that was fickle and false. As this feeling grew, it changed to one of resentment because I felt that my daughter and I were only necessary when my husband wanted to present this perfect family image to the world and to close family. It was as if we were just for show or display purposes; the rest of the time, we were unimportant.

So it was whilst I was sitting on the bale in Nancy's stable, watching Nadur take his first steps of his life, reflecting on the journey Nancy had taken me on, that it struck me that the focus hadn't changed from Nancy to me. In fact, her focus had always been on me; she had been healing me, giving me the tools to change my own life. I was gobsmacked with the realisation of this. Why had I not seen this before? I had set out determined to help and heal Nancy, but I now realised that I had been taken on a journey of discovery that led me down paths I would never have ventured. I had had my eyes and mind opened to countless weird and wonderful things, and I felt richer for it. Three years on, I was having a wonderful adventure that transformed how I looked at horses and how I worked with horses. I organically had healed and changed without knowing it! My self-worth and confidence had been so low, there was no way I would have faced training in something new to give me the means to support my daughter on my own. Through Nancy, though, I had found *me* again. I found a confidence in something I was doing, and it was becoming my new job which gave me financial security. Asked by friends to work on their horses and then friends of friends and so on, I got to the point that I was so busy, I needed to make a decision: to leave the stud and go full-time into bodywork or turn work away. I loved my newfound job, and it fit like a glove, as if I had been meant to be doing this all along. The turmoil in my private life and my years of self-doubt, however, kept rearing their heads. I kept asking myself, *Can I really do this? Am I good enough to do this?* I seemed to be forever not trusting in my own ability and sabotaging my path forward. I needed to sort this out. The turning point was when I helped Ginger Lucy and actually proved to myself in front of others that I could make a difference. I *was* good enough to do this! I *had* helped save her life, and I had seen it for myself, so no more excuses. With support and encouragement from Beth, Ellie, and my daughter, I took the leap into full-time equine bodywork therapy and separated from my husband. I have never looked back. Of course, Jacko played his crucial role as my biggest support and confidant. It's not easy talking to family or other people about private matters as emotional as a marriage breakdown, but I could tell Jacko everything. It's funny how I couldn't find the words to talk to humans, but I could pour my heart out to Jacko. I needed time with him; it was crucial. I couldn't wait for those precious stolen hours I would spend with him. He was my lifeline. Without him, I felt as if I would drown in the turmoil. I was devastated and heartbroken, then angry, confused, and fearful—ultimately lost. But I could be honest about all that to Jacko. I look back now and marvel at the fact that he didn't run and hide every time he saw me coming with all my woes! In fact, he always came over to me. Even when I just needed to sit in the field and stop, I would soon be joined by him doing exactly the same thing, just stopping and standing or lying down by me, letting me know I was not alone. He was such a wonderful rock, giving me strength with a tonic of laughter. Looking back, I see that he had been holding the space for me to heal, as he did with the kids, whilst Nancy encouraged me to explore new avenues. Their teamwork had gotten me through. The marriage broke down as I had awakened to what I was ignoring and how it was affecting me. I walked away from the business to save my sanity—not an easy decision after all the hard work to establish it. I finished fostering children. Divorce followed that. My escape route had been Nancy, and my support was Jacko. However, after Jacko's poisoning, whilst Nancy was busy being a mum, he had a few more things to show me before I could address this ability I seemed to have to allow myself to be ignored and made to feel worthless.

# CHAPTER 12

# WALKING

It took a lot of bodywork, fabulous care by my farrier to complete the growth of Jacko's new feet, and miles of walking in hand to develop Jacko's proprioception and get him moving normally again. When I began to ride him out, I chose to ride him bareback, which allowed me to really feel how he was moving. This became a great tool for knowing what he was struggling with and where he needed more help. We slowly worked at building his proprioception and fitness back up. It got to the point where he actually felt great everywhere except in his pelvis. One side felt free, but the other side felt jammed and sticky when I rode him. This didn't make sense as I had worked equally on both sides with the bodywork and he had regained his full range of motion in all limbs. His in-hand exercises and ridden work was again carried out evenly on both sides. He wasn't lame or compensating for anything that I was aware of, so why was this side of his pelvis not as free as the other side? Then it struck me that I was only aware of it when I rode him; he didn't seem to be jammed up when I worked him in hand. Years before, I had had a major pelvic injury, and now I began to wonder if it was me causing

Jacko's restriction. I got out my books on stretching and quickly established where I was restricted. Then I tried various stretching and strengthening exercises to free up my pelvis and even up the movement I had. You know what? Out of all the fancy exercise books, stretching books, and balance work, it turned out that walking was actually the key! Out with the dog one day, I did that horrid thing of stepping into a hole unexpectedly and jarring my lower back. It took my breath away. As I stood there gasping, I had a light-bulb moment. The passive moves I had used with the horses' front limbs to free up their range of motion also had given them their suspension back. My suspension was obviously nonexistent, so I needed to free it up with a passive move. I first took note of how I was walking and realised that I was bracing my lower back all the time and not allowing my pelvis to move freely at all. *A bit stupid,* I thought. *Why do I do that?* To rectify this, I played around with walking very slowly down hills. Every time I took a foot off the ground, I would allow that side of my pelvis to drop towards the floor using gravity alone—not a forced movement, but a passive/relaxed drop of the pelvis (simulating the passive movement technique I use on the horses). To my horror and discomfort, I found that my left side wouldn't drop and it was painful when I relaxed my lower back muscles to allow the drop. So I knew I needed to do a lot of this until it wasn't painful and it could drop the same as the other side, but it wasn't nice. The injury had been to my right side, but my left was now so tight that it hurt to get it moving. I had no idea I was so wonky until I did this. It took awhile, and I had to build it up to be able to do this, not only downhill but also on the flat, and then uphill, which was really hard. Uphill, you have to engage those dreaded core muscles to allow the back muscles to stay relaxed! I also realised that it all became much easier when I consciously made sure that I kept breathing. I think the anticipation of the pain made me hold my breath. When my pelvis was finally able to drop freely and evenly, both sides, there were two benefits. Firstly, Jacko remained free in his pelvis. Yippee! Secondly, if I happened to stand in a hole unexpectedly, my pelvis was able to absorb the concussion of the jarring step without that awful gasp-worthy pain that I used to experience. I used to laugh at the fact that at forty-something I was finally learning to walk properly. I must have looked like a flat-footed waddling duck before, huffing and puffing with the effort of walking!

So it was me all along who had been preventing Jacko's body from moving evenly. The pelvis is the structural part of the human body that touches a horse when we ride, so I guess it makes sense that the pelvis needs to be free of tension to allow the horse its full movement. If it isn't free of tension, then no matter how much one works on correcting the problem, one will have to keep adapting his or her own movement to compensate for the lack of movement. That never ends well, so I urge all horse riders to get some bodywork done or just pay attention to what restrictions they may feel in their own bodies. Like me back then, many riders I talk to have never given it a thought that their horses will be compensating for the human's restricted movement. It also taught me how I was so unaware a lot of the time of how much I was tensing my body unnecessarily. I think that if I weren't an equine bodywork therapist with the horses' constant reminders of this, I would be a bundle of tense muscle, unable to bend, sit, or straighten up by now. I still do my walking exercises and check in regularly with how even my pelvis is. I feel it's my absolute duty to keep my pelvis free of tension so I don't cause the horse to have to adapt when I ride. My back also feels so much better because of it, so it was a win-win! It never ceases to amaze me how the human–horse connection can work so well and positively help both parties.

# CHAPTER 13

# SPOOKY

There was one more lesson or eye-opening experience to have before Jacko departed from this physical world, and that was to do with distance healing. I had heard it discussed at the reiki course, and I'd had discussions with Sara K about it, but I couldn't get my head round the fact that someone could heal another living being without at least touching them or being in the same room. Then "Spooky Sara", as I fondly call her, opened my mind to it when she healed Jacko's left hind foot. I have never to this day met her or watched her work, but I have seen the results of her work, and I have no doubt that she can heal from a distance. Jacko had recovered well, but his left hind hoof never grew properly and was his weak point. If he went lame, it was always that hoof. It grew deformed on the outside wall, and he was prone to abscesses and bruising in the hoof frequently. The farrier tried to build it up with resin and shod him to give him more support. I tried riding him in boots and was always careful what ground he went on. However, eighteen months on and that hoof just wasn't growing properly and seemed weak, whereas the others were all fine, perfectly normal, healthy hooves. I contacted

Spooky Sara about Jacko as a last resort really. I know better now! I hadn't told her about his poisoning, just that he had had pedal bone rotation and laminitis two years prior. She said, "The problem is, the poison that caused it all damaged his digital blood vessel, so the hoof isn't getting enough blood supply, but I can try to fix that." I was literally speechless. You would think that after all the weird and wonderful adventures Nancy had sent me on, I would be used to the crazier, spooky stuff. How had Spooky Sara known about the poison? More importantly, how could she fix a blood vessel when she was one hundred miles away? I finally found my voice to ask how and when. She said to have Jacko in his stable at 3 p.m. on the Wednesday of that week and to sit quietly with him but not to touch him or interact with him. Her session would take approximately an hour, and then she would ring me when she was done to discuss her findings. So that was it. I was all set and ready on the Wednesday, and Jacko was eating hay quietly in his stable. I don't really know what I was expecting, but at 3 p.m. exactly, Jacko suddenly stopped eating. His head lowered towards the floor, and he looked like he was sleeping or in a trance-like state. It was just like Nancy during her reiki session. His lips and nose were twitching, and his eyes were nearly shut, as if he was relaxed and dreaming. In fact, his whole body was subtly twitching. He stayed like that for fifty minutes. He didn't move or shuffle his feet; he just stood twitching. Then at 3.50 p.m., he woke up, stretched, and continued eating as if nothing had ever happened. Spooky Sara phoned me to tell me she thought that the session had gone well, that Jacko needed to have plenty of fresh water and maybe some electrolytes, if I had any to hand, that night, and that I should keep him warm. Other than that, he should make a full recovery.

Now the only way to know if she had actually healed the blood vessel was to wait and see if the hoof began to grow normally. As you probably know, hooves take a long time to grow. So, to mark the day of the treatment, we drew a line in permanent marker on the top of the hoof under the coronary band where the new hoof develops, and then we waited. It was unbearable, the frustration of watching a hoof grow. The first few weeks, I was checking it all the time. Eventually, though, it was amazing to see that as his hoof grew and the line we had drawn moved down his hoof, the hoof below the line was all deformed, whereas the hoof above the line was growing perfectly normal. I didn't dare to believe it to begin with, but, yes, Spooky Sara had actually healed Jacko's hoof without being near him or even meeting him or me. His hoof grew out completely normally and he stopped getting abscesses from that day on. I am now a believer in distance healing. I have given Sara's number to many a friend and client over the years. I reasoned with myself that I don't really know how a mobile phone actually works, I just know it does. It's the same with distance healing. It helped my horse fully recover, so do I need to know how it works, not really. I'm just forever grateful that it does.

# CHAPTER 14

# FAREWELL

Jacko made a full recovery, and I was blessed with another five years of fun and laughter with him. He aged disgracefully with his partner in crime, a forty-plus-year-old Shetland pony called spider, getting up to all sorts of mischief and fun, causing mayhem whenever they could. But my wonderful, dear, sweet Jacko had to leave eventually. I was just driving home from work on a beautiful sunny November afternoon, enjoying the amazing show of autumn colours the trees were putting on for us, when a particular song came on the radio. It immediately took me back to times with Jacko. I could feel my fingers running the length of his soft roan-coloured neck and entwining with his silver mane. How I had held on to him, held on to my sanity, and held on to life. I hadn't ever wanted to let go. He had been my escape from the loneliness, from the heartache, from the pretence. He had helped me cry, then laugh, then cry some more. I had ridden him over hills and fields, tears streaming down my face, my vision blurred, but the thrill of his excitement was contagious. He had helped me forget everything just for a while, everything but the strength of his body, along with the power and the freedom he gave me. He had carried me. He held me together and helped me grieve, and then made sure I felt alive and loved. Although it's been three years since we said goodbye, I cried the whole duration of the song and then some! I miss him every day. I know it will be hard to write this chapter, but his passing was a very lovely farewell.

My homeopathic friend Sara K was able to turn a moment that we all dread into something that I now hold dear. The morning when I found Jacko standing in the field with evidence all about him that something was wrong and I saw he had not moved from that spot for several hours shook my world. Jacko and I had never communicated like Nancy and I had, but on that morning, it was like it had been with Sailor in Australia. I just knew it in my heart and could see it all over his face. He didn't need to tell me; I could feel it. He was ready to move on, and I needed to honour that. So without further ado, but with a very heavy heart, I made the arrangements, and with the remaining hours I had with him, I performed what I now call our goodbye ritual.

Sara gave me a spray bottle with some remedies in it that I was to spray on my hands and then slowly and gently rub all over Jacko, every part of his body. As I did this, a peculiar calm came over me, and Jacko relaxed and nodded his head. It's a beautiful thing, touch. Running my hand slowly down his body, I was casting to memory the shape of him, the colour of his coat, and the warmth of his body. I was able to thank this amazing horse for everything he had done. It gave me a job to do, a part to play in his final moments. It allowed the time for closure and took the pain and emotional sting out of it. It was like performing a ritual that made our time together feel complete. It was something I had never experienced before, and although it was still a very sad time for me, this ritual turned it into a memory that I hold very dear. I feel honoured to have experienced that with him. However, something went out inside me when he left; I kind of lost my rhythm, my bounce, for a while. And although at the time I didn't think his job was done, that I still needed him, I now see that he was right. I was ready to stand on my own two feet again, and thanks to him and Nancy, I was stronger than ever.

I was divorced now, had moved house, had built up my equine myotherapy business to full-time, and had supported my daughter through this massive change, along with her GCSE and A levels. She hadn't fallen off the rails yet and actually seemed very happy in our new life, so I couldn't ask for more than that. I was just beginning to get back into a rhythm after all the upheaval and Jacko's farewell, when the unimaginable happened: Nancy died! It had been only a matter of months since Jacko's departure, but Nancy wasn't coping well without him. She kept having frequent episodes of colic. Colic is defined as abdominal pain in horses, and can encompass several forms of gastrointestinal conditions which cause the pain. She was running around the field a lot more, the slightest thing upsetting her and setting her off around the field again. All this sudden extra movement was also aggravating her original injury and causing more pain. I couldn't touch her in places, and she couldn't relax enough to let me help. Coupled with the hormonal stress response (flight mode) within her body, the movement was causing the colic, but nothing I did seemed to settle her. I thought it would just be a matter of time to come to terms with the loss of Jacko—the same for all of us—but then one morning Nancy had a very serious bout of colic which resulted in her death. I hadn't wanted to make that decision for her, even though I could see she was distraught in the days leading up to it. It was just too close to Jacko's farewell; I couldn't say goodbye to her too. So in her own way, she took the decision out of my hands and forced the cards. It was quick and sudden, and such a stark contrast to the farewell I was able to have with Jacko. As a result, I still have unresolved feelings around her death. I felt cheated out of giving her the goodbye ritual. I felt guilty for not doing more for her sooner, and then I felt guilty that it all had happened too fast and for allowing her death. I felt numb for a long time afterwards and refused to even try to make sense of it. How could this have happened, both Jacko and Nancy leaving me just as things were looking so good? With so many changes and so much to look forward to now, this up and happened. It almost felt that they were jumping ship just as my life was piecing together, but how selfish was I to think that after all they had done? So I stopped thinking about it and buried the grief deep. It has been three years since Nancy left us, and I'm only now beginning to allow myself to open the wound and feel these feelings. To allow them to come to the surface is part of the process of writing this book, I guess. It is, however, very hard. I sit here with a box of tissues and a glass of water with ignatia in it, a homeopathic remedy for grief. For the first time, I think I can begin to accept that Nancy had known I wouldn't make the call, or couldn't make that call, so she did. Her job, too, was done. She had handed the baton to Nadur and had left. I miss her deeply.

Through Jacko, I navigated my divorce, witnessed and was an unwitting participant of the power of equine healing, found homeopathy, and learned to walk properly. Through Nancy, I changed my life and found my true self. I had my mind opened to explore the unusual, had found my new job, and had fallen in love with life again. It took a few years, but I also began to see how Nancy had mirrored where I was in my life back then, grief-stricken through my marriage breakdown and in a lot of physical pain. I had struggled with a painful problem in my pelvis that I could no longer ignore. I thought it was from an old injury, but unbeknown to me, there was a lot more going on than I was aware of at the time. Nancy may have finished her lessons for me, but Nadur picked up where she left off and became my next teacher. I was about to begin to learn true horse–human alignment, mirroring, and how horses know what is wrong with us before we do. Also, when Nancy gifted me with Nadur, I had no idea that I was about to begin the hardest lesson of all, that is to address self-limiting patterns of behaviour and emotions that can also manifest as physical pain in the human body. So before I talk about the lessons Nadur had for me, I want to talk about how I learned to take control of my thoughts and emotions to begin to change the self-doubt and sabotaging thoughts I always seemed to be up against. This in turn allowed me to understand what I have control over and what I don't have control over in my life and how that affects my physical body as well as my mental health.

# CHAPTER 15

# MENTAL HEALTH— IT'S A WAY OF LIFE

My studies of anatomy and physiology for the equine bodywork gave me the opportunity to learn about the hormonal processes within the body and what the fight or flight response actually translates to from a hormonal point of view. Animals such as horses that find themselves in a stressful situation experience a hormonal surge of cortisol, epinephrine (adrenaline), and norepinephrine, to heighten their responses to either flee (run away) or fight to survive. Along with other hormones and neurotransmitters such as dopamine and serotonin, these change the function of the brain to one of survival. The body's other functions become background to this, meaning that digestive function slows, immune function slows, growth slows, and all other functions that are not paramount to this acute survival mode slow, including cognitive functions that help one to learn. All the emphasis is on muscle function, increased heart rate, and respiratory function to allow for fight or flight. Knowing this, I can see how it is difficult for a frightened horse to learn or be healthy.

To have a calm, unstressed horse is to have a healthy horse that has the ability to learn. The horse's body can cope with such a hormone surge if it is genuinely only when it has had a random fright. In such a case, the horse will efficiently clear its body of those particular hormones and return all other body functions to a normal state relatively quickly. If the horse is living in a continued state of stress or fright, then its body will struggle to function normally as it is always producing too much of those stress hormones to allow the other body systems to function normally. This is also the same for *me*, I realised, as a human shares the same physiological make-up as a horse. So to keep my horses in an unstressed state is important, but it is equally as important that I remain in a nonstressful state, knowing that what I think about and feel emotionally is what controls the release of hormones in my body. Therefore, I need to be in control of my thoughts and emotions to stay healthy in my mind and body.

I was not in control of these and most definitely had not been in a stress-free environment. In fact, my whole life seemed to see me in situations surrounded by people who constantly undermined my self-worth and my confidence. I felt as if I always had to prove myself to people, to shout louder to be heard. Ironically, I also seemed to be attracted to putting myself in situations that meant I had to do exactly that. For example, I studied at an agricultural college on a course that had only six females out of one hundred and eight pupils. Working in Australia saw me trying to prove my worth not only as an Englishwoman in the outback but also as a female in a male-dominated environment. I met only one other jillaroo out there, but many jackaroos. I took on summer jobs in England that meant I was physically challenged to prove my worth. Grain-cleaning operations in Cornwall, Devon, and Somerset had me lifting 50 kg bags of cleaned and treated seed grain all day onto pallets and trailers. Most of the lads who came to try it out for a day failed at doing that! Whereas I determinedly charged ahead and coped, as if I were possessed. My business partners and my husband were the final straw, I think.

Mental health is a topic that keeps coming up more and more these days. I must admit that I didn't really understand it until I was forced to. Faced with divorce, reduced income, obliterated self-worth, and a young daughter to look after and support, I couldn't make sense of how I had ended up where I was or how I was going to get out of this mess. I couldn't talk to anyone about it either, even though I have wonderful parents and friends who I know would have tried to help me. I was in a weird mental state of stress-hormone-fuelled thinking, along with having the long-term overwhelming belief that I was a failure and not worthy enough to burden anyone else with my problems. I found it impossible to talk to anyone to begin with. I was faced with the mammoth task of not only coming to terms with the devastation of the situation, which was complicated further by the ties of our family business, but also of being the face of strength and assurance for my daughter. All I really wanted to do was to curl up and sob my heart out, then scream and shout with the anguish of the betrayal, then run away from the hurt and not look back. This emotional roller coaster I was riding, however, had to be hidden and concealed for the sake of my daughter and be replaced with the calming, consoling face of strength. She looked at me, her mum. If Mum is OK, then she is OK; if Mum is calm, then she has nothing to worry about; if Mum is carrying on with normal everyday stuff, then so can she. This was the hardest of all the tasks I had been handed. It was so very, very hard to do but so very, very, important for her sake.

Having to wear the mask of "everything is fine" to the outside world whilst being torn apart inside took me to a very dark and contorted place in my mind. I didn't know how I could best help myself to prevent a complete collapse of my inner self. It was a close call. I felt as if I'd fallen into this black pit of miserable despair where the sides were steep and slippery, and no matter how strenuously I crawled, I just kept slipping back in. In this lonely pit of dark negative thoughts, churning the same stuff over and over, I thought it was easier surely to just stay there and admit defeat, feeling worthless and very sorry for myself. At least I was at the bottom and couldn't fall any further, right?! But it was horrible in the pit, feeling as if I barely had a hold on reality. I was desperately close to losing the fragile grip I had in that dark pit. Being continuously triggered with so many strong emotional responses, I was close to losing it all. I couldn't think straight, and it was hard to even know where to start to rebuild my life. I knew my daughter really needed me, so she was my focus, but honestly, without Jacko already in my life as my rock, and then Nancy turning up right then amidst all the turmoil to give me focus, I'm not sure I would have made it out of that slippery pit at all. They helped to stop the emotional roller coaster and allowed me to step off it occasionally. It took me a long time to get out of the pit and be able to stay out of it, but that was because I didn't know then how to take control of my mind and my thoughts and break the pattern I was in. There was too much to try to sort out and make sense of, and too many strong emotions always rearing their heads to allow clear thought. I would focus on changing just one thing first to at least make a start. I would get a little confidence from that and start to feel that maybe I could do this, maybe I would get us through this. But then some other problem would take its place, or a conversation would upset me, triggering emotions, and then it would feel as if all the walls had crumbled again. I would slide straight back into the pit, wallowing around in pity and self-doubt, and spend hours dwelling on all the negatives in my life and blaming others for where I was. This happened time and time again, my fragile progress out of the pit and then slipping back down to the bottom again. It was only when I had repeated this more times than I can count that I got really angry with myself for having allowed it. *For goodness's sake, I must surely be able to change this somehow? Why can't I change this pattern? I know I want to.* But it was as if my brain was just forcing me to keep reacting this way to any little upset, and then I'd find myself in that bloody pit of darkness, where everything seemed so pointless and unattainable for someone like me.

Beth gave me a book to read one day. The book she gave me intrigued me enough to set me on a path on which I eventually learned how to get control of my thoughts, how to recognise when my thoughts were falling into the negative, and how to stop them from doing so and purposely change them to positives. It was an absolute lifesaver for me. It was also the first time I had come across *The Law of Attraction*, which prompted me to read more and more books to get a real understanding of the power I had to change everything I was getting in life.

It was about being very conscious of everything I was thinking and also of what I was saying, the words I used, and the emotions I felt as I said those words and thought them. The whole point was not to give thought to the things I didn't want but only to the things I wanted. At that point in my life, I felt that there were far more negatives outweighing the positives, so this would be tricky. As I began to take note of what I was thinking of all the time, it became apparent to me very quickly what my biggest problem was: I wasn't aware when I began to dwell on the negative things. I can honestly say that for me it took at least eighteen months to really become aware of each time my thoughts, words, and emotions turned to negative. It used to frustrate the hell out of me to suddenly realise that for the past twenty minutes I had allowed my mind to dwell on a topic that upset me, angered me, or lowered my emotional energy and that it had taken twenty minutes for me to even realise it.

I decided that the only way I was going to stay out of that pit was to control everything around me that I had the ability to control and to bombard myself with positive thoughts. I found I needed to stop watching the news or reading newspapers. I became very careful about what I read and listened to. I only socialised with people who I knew would be more likely to focus on having fun and laughing a lot and who only talked about positive things, not allowing myself to be dragged into conversations that had negative emotions attached to them, anger, pity, guilt, fear, and worry to name a few. I bought a mug that had bumps on it, and each morning I would feel for the bumps. For each bump I felt, I would find something to be grateful for. I called this my "gratitude mug", and I still use it today. I would write down words or quotations that I would repeat through the day to bring my thoughts back to where I wanted them to be and break the old patterns of unconscious thoughts taking over. This is how I personally began the task of changing my subconscious conditioned responses to everything in my life. As my stress hormone levels reduced and my state of mind changed, I was able to talk to my parents, my brother Jon, and a few close friends, which made a huge difference. The leap forward I made then was massive. The support of family and friends is so important; together my family and friends formed a net underneath me, which I never needed to fall into, but to know it was there was very, very comforting.

There are loads of books out there written in varying degrees of complexity on the topic of mental well-being, psychology, positive thought, and very importantly the law of attraction. The ones I have read (I have listed some of them at the end of the book) helped me to understand how my mind really functions and how my emotions are crucial to my thought process and behavioural responses. Emotions give power to a thought and trigger the hormonal reactions in our bodies. The stronger the emotion, the more powerful the thought. The strongest emotions are anger, fear, resentment, and hate, along with love and joy. As you can see, a lot of the negative emotions are the strongest, so negative thoughts tend to have more power behind them. That's why it was easier for me to remember the few unpleasant things than it was to remember all the everyday pleasant things going on in my life. I was putting a lot of energy into my negative thoughts about my situation. The law of attraction holds that what you put out multiplies and comes back to you. All that energy going out there to create more negatives was coming right back at me. Why would I want to allow that?

I took control of my thoughts and so, by default, got control of my emotional responses. I changed the way I responded to most situations and ultimately improved my mental and physical well-being. So now I was attracting what I wanted into my life, and not what my uncontrolled reactions attracted. I broke the negative patterns and really changed my future. I have never revisited that pit of misery. It was hard work, and it was relentless in the beginning, but I truly wanted to make those changes and was prepared to keep working at it. It did become so much easier with practice and repetition. Soon I realised that I hardly needed to check myself. This way of controlled thinking became the *conditioned* response. I write about this in the hope that if, God forbid, you should ever find yourself in the pit, you may learn to climb out of it quicker than I did. It turns out I was stronger than I knew and that there is life after divorce! In fact, I came through all that crap and am now stronger, happier, and smarter. I write about this also because it was a big part of what has shaped me into becoming who I am today. I had to learn about my weakness of mind in order to begin to learn how to strengthen my mind. I had been attracting the people and scenarios into my life that kept my (negative) beliefs about myself alive. I attracted the people and scenarios that ultimately reinforced the belief that I was less important and not worthy. I was extremely fortunate to have Jacko and Nancy in my life to support me and guide me through this growth. Because of them, I am not just surviving; I am thriving. As I progressed along this path of changes, I also began to realise that as I am the only one in charge of my mind, then it follows that I am the only one responsible for how I react to, interpret, and respond to any experience I have. Therefore, I am the only one responsible for everything I have gone through. I cannot blame anyone else any more. I cannot pass the buck any more. I chose to interpret everything in that way and therefore chose to react in that way. I have to take that responsibility, accept it, and be OK with it. My mission now was to understand where those long-term negative beliefs about myself worth had come from in the first place.

When Nadur began to teach me, I had my mind in a better place to learn his lessons. I had definitely made it out of that pit and had mastered being aware of where my thoughts were leading me and what they were attracting into my life. I had made huge inroads to being able to control which emotions I allowed to be dominant, giving power to positive thoughts instead of negative ones. I had also dealt with a lot of the emotional trauma of the past few years, particularly the anger—or so I thought! In fact, Nadur was about to show me that all I had done was to bury the emotions deeper and save it all for later. He was about to address the fact that this emotional trauma was stored in my body, just like physical trauma can be, and that it was causing me physical pain in my pelvis and lower back. I needed help to let this go. He was my help. And the hardest lessons yet were about to begin.

# CHAPTER 16

# NADUR—LESSON 1

Nadur was born jet black with a white blaze and an air of absolute confidence and ease in his own power. Knowing his own mind, he was strong-willed and embraced change and new discoveries easily, almost eagerly. Nadur had had a wonderful start in life; he was part of a big herd, which included his mum, Nancy, for the first four years of his life. He changed colour from black to pale grey with a darker band around his middle. Eventually he turned whiter and developed dapples, losing his black mane and tail for white ones. He is like a chameleon; changing his colour and markings each season. He learned how to be a horse, learning herd rules and etiquette with plenty of playtime. However, he was a colt, so he was also taught to interact with humans politely and safely. For the most part, he was a lovely young horse to handle and be around.

The first lesson I was to learn from Nadur began when he was just months old. He would stealthily come up behind me, or any unsuspecting human for that matter, and bump me in the back with his chest. This, at first, I took to be just the usual dominant colt behaviour, pushing boundaries, testing to see what he could get away with. Then I began to notice that he didn't do it when I was staying present and focused with him. I had just begun my journey of learning to be aware of where my thoughts were, but my mind was all over the place most of the time, with thoughts of other things I had to do that day or worries over personal stuff and family matters. I was literally more in my head and not in the present moment. First lesson: always stay present and focused with him; never get distracted. If I was to venture into his world (be it the field or stable), he demanded I give my full awareness to him and be present in that moment. I watched time and time again as he did this to friends and family who came to visit. They had all been warned, by the way, but had all clearly lost focus very quickly (typically human), chatting to each other, not present in what they were actually doing in that moment. He very quickly taught them the lesson and would continue to teach them until they really got the message. A dear friend of mine was bumped four times before she got the message. We still laugh about it now as she has never forgotten the lesson. She remains present with him when she visits—and with all her own horses too! Once the lesson had been learned, Nadur was very polite and obliging and respected our space. My thoughts on it were, why shouldn't he demand my full attention/awareness when I am the one entering into his world? I expect his full attention and cooperation when he is brought into my world for the farrier or vet, or just being led from stable to field. I felt this lesson in being mindful in the present moment was a fair lesson indeed.

The only person Nadur never did this to was a little boy who came to stay with me. This particular boy had come from a violent and abusive home, and he carried a lot of anger and fear. Nadur was only a few months old and already proving to be quite the dominant colt foal, but when this boy entered the field or stable, I would witness extraordinary interactions between these two. For one, this little boy had never been near horses, but his gentleness towards them was utterly mind-blowing, bearing in mind that he had wild rages and aggressive tendencies towards humans—adults and children alike. For the most part, he displayed utter dislike and distrust towards humans. However, his whole demeanour would change when around my horses; his eyes would soften and come alive. I guessed that living in a violent world, he had developed his awareness to a more heightened level than most of us need to do (the particular lesson that Nadur was teaching me). He could read body language like a horse, and even the subtle changes didn't go unnoticed by this super-aware little boy. Nadur had no need to teach him that lesson. What he did do, though, was to respect the boy with utter gentleness. Nadur would act completely out of character for a colt foal, respectfully lowering his head when approaching this boy (from the front) and then allowing the boy to rest his forehead on his own forehead. They would stand like that for minutes at a time, forehead to forehead, just standing there in silent gentle respect. I, however, would be having an internal meltdown at this point. Anyone who knows what it's like to have a very colty foal to handle will understand the speed at which the teeth and front legs can be unleashed to lethal effect. Couple that with an aggressive, angry boy—well, you can see my quandary! To my utter astonishment, though, never once did Nadur raise a leg or try to bite. In fact, I became aware that it was Nadur instigating this whole gentle, respectful contact.

There was without a doubt some amazing healing in this display of absolute gentleness from a very powerful, dominant character like Nadur. This particular boy needed so much of it, and Nadur gave it freely. Every morning before the boy went to school, whilst we were doing the stables, this connection/healing usually occurred. Afterwards, the probability of this boy's making it through the whole day at school without running away or attacking someone increased dramatically. It became part of his day, and it set him up for success. I was in awe of this young horse and how he was so determined to help us humans heal.

# CHAPTER 17

# ALL ABOUT THE FEET!

The second lesson was much harder to learn though, and I only really worked it out with the help of a man I will call Adam. After Nadur had been backed as a three-year-old, he came home very angry and aggressive towards me. This saddened me and worried me, but it is a big ordeal for a lot of young horses when they first start their work under saddle, so I decided to give him time to think and grow. He went back with the herd for another year. During that year, he lost Jacko, then his mum, and also had to move to a new yard—a lot of emotional changes. When I began to work him in hand, Nadur, now a four-year-old, was proving to be very difficult. He would bite and threaten to kick. He would try to squash me and push me around. It even escalated to the point where he would rear up and box at me with his front feet. When I took him into the school, he would do what we call the "wall of death", which means the horse runs flat out in a circle around you and you have no control or communication with it at all. Horses in this state run blindly as fast as they can. It's not good; the potential for injury is huge to horse and human alike.

Adam came to see Nadur and promptly told me that I was misreading a lot of Nadur's body language, adding that it was starting in the stable before I even got a halter on him. For example, when I walked into his stable, Nadur would politely step back as he had always been taught, but he would then step forward ever so slightly with one hind foot only. I would miss this, and in Nadur's mind this was confirmation that he was in control of his own feet. Adam made it very clear that I was not, in any way, in control of my horse's feet and that this was the only problem I had. What? He was saying that if I were to get control of his feet, all the other disagreeable behaviour would disappear!

Horses live their lives with this sole rule: whoever moves the other's feet is the boss. So Nadur not only was in control of his own feet but also had taken control of my feet! When he got away with his little test of moving his hind foot subtly, he would then try to bite me, which would see me jump out of the way (who wouldn't, right?). He was the boss because he could move my feet. As boss horse, he was allowed to bite, kick, and shove if he so chose. Adam told me that a horse wouldn't dare bite or kick the boss horse; in fact, just the flick of an ear or a look from the boss horse is enough to make the other horses move their feet—and quickly.

Right, so how do I get control of his feet?

Adam introduced me to the flag on the end of his schooling whip. *OMG, he thinks I'm going to let him beat Nadur with his flag!* I thought. Then I watched as Adam didn't even go into the stable but just stood outside the box. And every time Nadur made a step forward, Adam would just shake the flag. To begin with, Nadur flew to the back of the stable, snorting. However, he got bold quite quickly and tried all ways to move or to move Adam, but Adam was on to him. Quite quickly, Nadur realised that Adam was definitely in control of his feet. Nadur could not make Adam move either! Every time Nadur stayed still, he got rewarded with Adam ceasing to shake the flag. Simple. Adam then went in to put the halter on and led Nadur out of the stable and down to the school. This took about fifteen minutes because Nadur tried all his usual things, barging, pulling, cutting Adam up, and biting. Adam stayed calm and just shook his flag, which made Nadur back up every time he did something undesirable. It is a simple, gentle, but effective tool. Nadur was being moved and failing to move Adam. When in the school finally, Nadur did his grand trick of rearing up and boxing, but Adam was already a step ahead and had raised the flag above his head (he is quite a tall chap) and was shaking it wildly in the air. This made him taller than Nadur. Nadur's eyes popped out of his head. The result was that he couldn't get his feet on the ground quickly enough, and he backed right up, away from Adam. He only tried it once more, and then that was that, no more rearing!

I had a go with the flag. Adam coached me in spotting all the subtle tests and things I had been missing. Basically anytime Nadur moved a foot, if I hadn't asked him to move, he got flagged, and I only stopped shaking the flag when he stayed put himself (or parked as I like to call it) where I wanted him. Adam also pointed out that I was unaware of how many times Nadur had moved me, albeit not my feet but my body, to avoid his teeth! For example, when he reached forward to bite me, I unknowingly moved my head and upper body away from his teeth. I had to be more body aware and never allow Nadur to move on me like that. That meant keeping him at a distance for a while so I had time to learn to control my reactions—much easier now with the flag.

These two simple awarenesses changed both Nadur and me so much that it wasn't long before I noticed the biting had ceased and the pushy manners and aggressive behaviour had all but vanished. He tested me every day and every minute I was with him to begin with, but I stayed consistently aware of our feet and my body position, and we have never looked back. To begin with, I had to allow a lot more time to do simple things such as walk him to his field because he tested me continuously, and so it would take a lot longer to walk fifty yards. But with my knowing this and planning for it, understanding what was going on, and having the tools now to deal with it, we got through it. I had learned lesson two thoroughly. Adam had said to me that Nadur is obviously a natural leader, quite dominant/confident, and that for the next couple of years I would have to be firm and consistent about these two things; otherwise, he would take control again very quickly. Adam was right, although Nadur doesn't behave this way as frequently—and never aggressively—now (two years on), but he does still test me occasionally, and when he does, he still gets the same answer from me. It took a few months before I was confident enough to allow him to work really close in hand (within biting distance), but again Adam was right in that once I had control of Nadur's feet, I found that all the unpleasant behaviour had fallen away. Nadur was respecting me as the boss horse now. This carries through into the ridden work too. If he moves without my permission, he gets put back where I wanted him. His reward is that when he parks, I cease everything; when he moves when I ask, I don't nag him. It is so ingrained now, my conditioned response when around horses, that I hardly need to think about it. I also feel safer around some of my clients' horses when at work. I interact with them in this way—their way—and they respond accordingly. Some respond more quickly than others, but it keeps me safer and them calmer too. Calmer because it's in their language and not done with anger or aggression towards them. I'm not bullying them; I'm just talking to them in the language they understand, so they don't need to fear me. A horse moving away out of fear is a very unpredictable horse; a horse moving away with respect is safe and calm. I don't take my flag with me to see every horse I go to; that would be a bit much, I think. Just being aware of the two rules, however—who is moving whose feet, and staying mindful of my body language—has seen a dramatic change in how clients' horses work with me when I'm doing bodywork, especially the young ones and bargy ones. Nadur is a fantastic teacher. It's what he does. I thank him every day for the lessons he gives. I also acknowledge that he had to be very dramatic to get my attention. I'm not the quickest at seeing things I need to address, and I wouldn't have had to get help or learn these lessons if he had been half-hearted in his actions. He is the most polite and responsive horse now that I can lead him anywhere in hand safely, no matter what we come across. I have walked him miles and miles in hand around the countryside, and he never pulls on the lead rope or runs over me. I hardly need to have hold of the rope as he is so in tune with my feet. When I stop or go, he stops and goes! He has gone from being a nightmare to being a dream horse, and all because of my mindfulness of my body language and our feet.

# CHAPTER 18

# DIAL IT DOWN!

By now I was feeling that Nadur and I could really understand each other, not on a "hearing words or seeing pictures in my head" kind of way, but just by being body aware. It's a two-way thing. Although initially I had to really work at being the boss horse in his language, I was doing it without aggression, anger, or force. Consistency and mindfulness of body language was all I had to master. However, my next lesson was to be in being aware of my energy as well as my body language. Having taken courses in kinesiology and reiki, I had been told a few times that my energy was strong, whatever that meant. Now I had to become aware of how this was making the horses I worked with feel.

I was at my dear friend Liz's home in Normandy, the home of Normandy Equine. I was taking part in a trial clinic she was running. Joining us were other friends and colleagues. Liz begins her lessons with shoulder alignment and talking about the importance of teaching the horse how to stay centred between its shoulders to prepare for ridden work. We had spent a morning learning the theory behind her work and then had gone outside to do some in-hand work with her horses.

Liz's horses all became quite animated when I was asked to work with them in hand on the first day. Liz said, "Boy, your energy is so high that I can feel it from here, Helen. You need to get control of that and dial it down." I had no idea what she meant. I was just going about my task in my usual fashion. I just looked at her blankly. Her horses, she explained, were showing me very clearly that my energy was way too high for them as they were trying to match it. I had to concentrate hard to dial it right down for them so they could work with me in a calmer fashion; I'd do this by using some breathing techniques as well as intent. This was really hard for me because I was unaware that I operated like that all the time. After all, I had always been like that. It took me awhile to be able to focus on the task at hand whilst keeping my energy levels lower—not natural for me at all. The other women were smiling and laughing at this as it came as no shock to them that this was my problem. What? They agreed that they themselves felt like the horses sometimes after I had been with them, visiting or working. They went on to say they would get worn out trying to match my energy. Not in a bad way, but still in a way that I was blissfully unaware of! I couldn't believe that none of them had ever mentioned this to me before. *Wow*, these comments made me stop and think of Nadur and me. Was I causing Nadur to react in a similar way (he was always bouncing and whizzing around) but I'd been unaware of it all this time? So, although we all had a good laugh about it and I was able to practise tempering my energy levels enough to work with Liz's horses nicely, I realised then I had found my next lesson.

As if to push the point further, I had another hot reminder whilst I was staying with Liz, this one a reminder of my energy and the ability I have to sense others' energies. Although I had stayed with Liz before, I had never slept upstairs on the third floor in the old part of her house. This is where her son sleeps when he is home from his studies. As he was away, she had put the yoga instructor in his bedroom. I was in the spare room next door. Each night we left the windows open because of the heatwave we were experiencing; the cool air was a welcome flow over our weary bodies. However, on night 3 I concluded that I was definitely under attack because each night so far, at around two o'clock, I had awakened sweating, really overheating, and very aware of another presence in my room. Of course there was no visible body in my room when I turned the light on, but my bedroom door had been opened and was now wide open. It actually felt as if my energy was under attack, as if whomever or whatever it was in my room was after my energy, and my own body was fighting it off and overheating from the effort. This would wake me at the same time each night. On that third night, I was still trying to convince myself that it was just because the weather was so warm and not to be so silly, so I shut the bedroom door, jammed the suitcase against it, and tried to go back to sleep. The door opened again, I was still awake, so I heard the suitcase moving as the door opened wide. I put all the lights on, put my music on loud with my headphones on, and sang to myself for the rest of night so as not to fall asleep again and allow another attack. Somehow I knew I was OK if I was awake.

In the morning, feeling wiped out but victorious, I spoke with Liz about this. She told me that she had felt things brush past her at times in the house and that another friend of hers had sensed an energy in the house, so she wasn't surprised to hear of my encounter. She was, however, quite alarmed at how it made me feel, as if it was trying to siphon my energy. Her son was always falling ill with asthma and other allergies such as hay fever when he came over. Was he under attack too?

Months before this, I had put Liz in touch with Spooky Sara as one of her horses needed help, so after the clinic was over, Liz contacted Sara and explained the situation, asking if it was something she could help with. Spooky Sara agreed to try and was able to help the entity move on. Alice was her name apparently, and she had lived in the house for many years but had unfinished business there holding her back. She *had been* siphoning energy from me, as she had been doing from Liz's son all these years, not maliciously, but to weaken us so she could then assume a caring role. She moved on quietly with Sara's help. Interestingly, since then, Liz's son has never had his allergies return when he stays at home! Truly spooky stuff, right?!

When I got back home, I watched carefully to see the way Nadur responded to me when I had changed only my energy levels and nothing else whilst working him. Sure enough, he was loud and clear: the answer was yes; my energy was absolutely causing changes in his energy levels. Pretty cool, really! But then I realised in shock that he had been shouting it to me for months. I just hadn't understood what he was trying to tell me. His energy levels had always been high, and I thought it was just him. *Wrong!* Now I know he was just matching my own level of energy. Once I began to really get to grips with controlling my energy when I was working with him, boy, we got on very well. I swear, I heard him sigh with relief several times!

I struggled with this issue of high energy for months before it began to get easier. If anything went wrong or Nadur was particularly playful (or I was being particularly confusing to him), my natural response was to kick into high energy. Eventually, after months of working with this in mind, I found that I could actually use it to my advantage. Most of Nadur's work at the moment is done with lower energy; however, if I dial it up, I can instantly get a change in him. This is going to be very useful later on in our work. He is very sensitive and reminds me frequently when I'm getting carried away to just rein it in a little. He tells me things all the time. Thank God I've learned the lessons so far which have helped me to listen to him. Having been forced to become so much more aware of body language, I see the changes so much more quickly now. He has pulled muscles in his side, had growing pains causing discomfort under saddle, and had many other normal and abnormal things happen to him. Every time his subtle body language has changed, and I have stopped and investigated, only to find each time that there was a very real reason for it. He has never had to resort to bucking, rearing, or being aggressive; we just work at having a mutual agreement to listen to each other without blame or upset. We both get things wrong frequently, but that is OK too, as long as we keep trying to listen. I soon began to notice how this lesson had filtered through into my work with clients' horses subconsciously. I am now able to stay energy-calm when working with very sensitive horses and their very sensitive humans.

CHAPTER 19

# PARALLELS

Before Nancy had changed my life, I mentioned that I had worked at a stud. Ellie had unwittingly thrown me a lifeline, which turned out to be my escape route from my family business in the retail world and my marriage. That business world and the people I had to associate with as a result, along with my husband, had so confirmed to me my low self-worth that I had shut down parts of myself and developed coping mechanisms in my behaviour. These patterns of behaviour in certain circumstances had become so ingrained that I was, for the most part, blissfully unaware that I had developed them. More alarmingly, I still used them years later. However, I was forced to become aware of them by Nadur and by the fact that my body was not coping well under their weight. This was shutting me down physically with pain.

Although I had come a long way on the path of healing and learning through my horses, every year around the same time, I would seemingly injure my back. Why was this? It happened always when work got really busy, when I was juggling mum duties with clients' needs, plus attending to the needs of my horses, dogs, cats, and family. Basically because I was trying to please everyone and not let people down, my lower back would shriek with pain and seize up. I would be out of action for a week at a time. It was agony and really not good for my business. I hadn't noticed this pattern myself, even though it had been there for several years now. A friend of mine, Kelly May, pointed it out to me one day when I was lying incapacitated on my sofa. A chance meeting at a client's yard had seen Kelly May and me become friends; we shared similar thoughts on how we wanted to be with our horses. We would have lengthy discussions about the weird and wonderful world of the equine and how we had both had our eyes opened to a bigger picture when it came to our horses. She began to come and help me with Nadur on occasions. Her unique ability is to help horses clear out emotional crap that they take on from us humans. She can feel it in her own body, so she knows where they are holding it. I love watching her work with horses. I see them release this emotional weight and then change in demeanour.

Nadur is a complicated and very sensitive character and cannot tolerate (in his view) unjust human behaviour from anyone, including me, or the farrier, or the horse dentist. As a young horse, he would hold onto that emotion and become restricted by it. Kelly May would help him to clear it. It's fascinating to watch, but also hugely beneficial for me to understand this about his character so I can understand him better.

Kelly May called in that day. As I lay on my sofa in agony, she saw that I could barely move. She asked me, "How often does this happen?"

I said, "Once a year, around now." After quite a lengthy discussion, she told me she had been going to something called "network spinal analysis" for years and that, like me, she had once had debilitating patterns of pain and restrictions in her body, but these now no longer troubled her. Basically what I began to understand was that my body had been conditioned to react to the feeling of this building pressure of trying to please everyone or trying not to let anyone down by seizing up my back in agony to stop me. The pain was to make me stop and listen, but I had done the usual thing of taking pain relief, resting my back for a while, and then ignoring it and carrying on for another year until it all happened again. I never addressed the real problem, which was the emotional issue underlying my back pain— the need to please everyone else. *Why?* Well, I was afraid of people thinking badly of me for letting them down. This saw me right back to my low self-worth issue. To make myself feel better, I tried to keep everyone else happy so they wouldn't see me as being somehow less than them, but all at the detriment to myself. What a crazy, messed-up tangle, confusing as hell to start with. My mind fought it for a few months. Not surprisingly. I now had to get my head around the idea that my patterns of behaviour and deeply rooted beliefs about myself, particularly ones I thought I had dealt with, not only were self-limiting but were also manifesting as physical pain in my body. The more I thought about it, the more intrigued I became. Ultimately, I really, really did want to be rid of this whole bloody low self-worth issue that kept coming up. To be rid of the crippling physical pain would be great too. In so many ways I was not only surviving but also thriving in life now, and I felt physically great most of the time, but I could definitely see that this was a pattern and one that needed to be stopped.

Was there really a way to help my own body change the way it was reacting when it recognised a trigger scenario such as a certain feeling (perceived pressure to prove my worth) or a certain experience/environment? Well, the only way to find out was to begin the most absolute pattern-breaking journey of my life so far—and Nadur stepped up and helped me.

CHAPTER 20

# AWAKEN

To explain the experiences I had along my network spinal analysis journey is difficult because that journey has changed my whole way of thinking about my body. The memories and physical traumas that I revisited as my body let them go were extraordinary. Over the first twelve-week period, I had memories pop into my head that I hadn't really thought about in years, some from back in my really early childhood and others more recent. Some may have been the seed for the low self-worth issues, and they stirred up some strong emotions. My body at times felt as if it had been through a mangle; it ached and shouted at me. Other times I felt like I was gliding about effortlessly, full of joie de vivre. Once I even experienced my left leg just refusing to work; it would just give way when I tried to use it to bear my weight. I remember I was given some simple breathing techniques to correct this. *Really?* I thought. *My leg is actually not working, and they want me to breathe!* I did, however, follow the instructions. Sure enough, an hour later my body had processed what it needed to process and my leg was perfectly fine—incredible and unbelievable! Also, it's very empowering to know that I can help my body adjust by doing some simple breathing techniques and really feeling the affected part of my body. I learned to acknowledge each strange reaction for what it was, letting go of either physical trauma memory or emotional trauma associated with a memory that has shaped my behaviours. The most bizarre thing was that I knew exactly what each reaction was related to. I was also able to help my body release these reactions—with the help of homeopathic remedies. For instance, when my body let go of three serious concussions I'd had in my younger life, I experienced the symptoms of each one in turn and therefore knew which incident was leaving my body. Unpleasant but fascinating, and similar to the kinesiology trauma release technique I had performed on my sister-in-law years ago! I had struggled throughout my life with bad headaches and migraine, but since my body let those traumas go, I have not had a headache since—except from indulging in too much gin from the local distillery! It is very good.

I had moments of ecstatic joy for no particular reason, along with moments of crushing tiredness, and once I actually passed out on my sofa for three hours in the middle of the day following a particularly powerful NSA session. My body was already feeling different—subtly different—and comfortable. I had experienced enough changes in those first twelve weeks to continue the journey. My NSA therapist told me I was progressing well and that my body was now working on female energy: the energy of not having a voice, not being able to say what I wanted to, or not being listened to. *Oh no,* I thought, *this is going to get heavy.* My not wanting to come across as a failure was also part of this, I guessed, as my body began to throw up the feelings and the traumas related to the feelings. I awoke really early one Friday morning and could feel my left shoulder and back tighten really painfully, so I adopted a pose to really feel it and began to do some breathing into the pain. The pain moved into the pectoral muscles across my chest, so I continued with the breathing exercises and then lay there for an hour. An amazing force of energy surged through my whole body, and as I lay there buzzing, a poignant memory popped into my head:

I had been working in Australia in the Queensland outback as jillaroo for a family on a forty-eight-thousand-acre station. We were in the middle of the big muster-up of sheep and cattle, so we were riding every day for eight to nine hours and driving the animals back to holding corrals at the property's centre. It was hot, hard work, and our regular mounts had tired, Sailor being mine, so the fresh horses were brought in from the back paddock. I hadn't even known there were spare horses out there. They hadn't been used for a couple of years, so they really were quite fresh. I was given Mort, who promptly rodeoed my arse off. I mean, he really rodeoed like a wild horse. As I sailed through the air, I had time to think, *This is going to hurt.* It did hurt. We didn't have hard hats out there, just our Akubra hats. The latter have life-saving qualities of their own, but they gave no protection when falling from a height. The sound it makes in your head when you land head first onto concrete-hard ground is horrid. The pain paralysed me momentarily, and the blackness threatened to overwhelm. I broke four ribs and concussed myself terribly, and I had other bruised body parts from having been thrown around in the saddle like a rag doll first. Those Australian stock saddles are great for all-day riding, but they hold you in too long when things go wrong like that. I was in a male-dominated workplace, and a shy Englishwoman to boot, so I picked myself up, brushed off the dirt, and got back on the horse without saying a word. I completed seven hours of ridden work (which I can barely remember), and then I had to try to dismount. The pain was unbelievable; I had nearly passed out a couple of times during the day already. Having to build myself up to the task of dismounting, I nearly passed out again when I finally got off. Mort did redeem himself a little by standing stock-still whilst I clung to his side for dear life whilst the pain screamed inside my body. I saw to my other chores before going into supper and getting some much-needed sympathy from Di, the wife and mother of the family, along with some very strong painkillers. I was a funny colour, she said! I was back in the saddle early the next morning with much the same pain and much the same result. Not one to make a fuss or let the team down at this critical time, I just quietly suffered, really suffered, and got on with my job. I still have a large dent in my ribcage where the ribs healed wonkily.

This memory fascinated me in the light of my not wanting to say anything to anyone about the pain I was in. It was about not coming across as a failure to the all-male team. Funny, that! I realised too that there was some other feeling lurking deep in this memory. It was as if I had no right to make a fuss. This was the first time this had come up. It wasn't to be the last either; I'll come back to this later. As my body worked at letting this emotional response go, I was also reliving a small amount of the pain incurred in that particular incident. I had landed on the top of my head and left shoulder after all!

As I continued with the NSA work, I soon began to notice that I was reacting differently to situations and to people. There was a calmness growing deep inside me, and I liked that. I could see that my body was literally unravelling, letting go of layers of unnecessary baggage. I was told I didn't need to analyse what my body was doing if I didn't want to, but that's not me. Of course I was going to want to understand it. A lot of times it was Nadur and Kelly May who helped me to understand what my body needed to let go of. I wouldn't come to appreciate the connections between Nadur and this journey—the parallels as I call them—without Kelly May. She has a wonderful ability to see things differently. A good example of this is the day I turned Nadur loose in the school to work with him at liberty and got a completely different horse from normal.

I had taken him into the school and let him go free, something I often did. I like to work him this way sometimes to give him the choice of staying or leaving. It gives me a good indication of the connection between us. I have gotten so very used to him staying with me and working with me, as if I have an invisible line attached to him, that I was utterly shocked that day as he galloped as fast as he could to the other end of the school and wouldn't look at me. I walked towards him, and he galloped past me again to the other end with his head thrown away from me as if he couldn't bear to look at me. He then stood there with his back to me. This is something I had never seen from him before, so I knew it was something I was doing or feeling that was causing it. It upset me and made me feel quite uncomfortable. We carried on in this manner for about ten minutes with no change; he absolutely refused to acknowledge me. I decided to return him to his field, promising him that I would think on this and try to figure out what the hell he was trying to tell me. I was thinking that with all the weird and wonderful memories and emotions coming up for me through the NSA work, I must be very uncomfortable to be around. However, Kelly May pointed out there was another way to look at it. She asked me, "What do you do to protect yourself from people you dislike, people in the past who made you uncomfortable or hurt you?" Aha! The penny had dropped. Nadur had been very clearly mirroring me, displaying exactly the thing I had done to protect myself back then. I blanked people—wouldn't look at them—and either moved away physically or energetically blocked them out (i.e. blanked them). I refused to acknowledge them if the circumstances were such that I could. But how the hell did Nadur know that? Kelly May then explained how she, too, had observed me doing this very thing, even in a group of people whom I knew and in a place where I felt comfortable and safe. I had sat in my protective bubble and made it difficult for my friends/colleagues to chat to me. OMG, I had no idea I was still doing that—no idea at all. I was shocked that I could do that and not know I was doing it, for goodness' sake! What else was I doing that I was not aware of? I needed to work at changing this because now it was preventing me from moving on. Nadur had made me feel quite uncomfortable, in fact. I guess that is how I'd made others feel at times. There have been many occasions in the past at different social gatherings when I have felt like a pariah and wondered what the hell was wrong with everyone. Now I know it was me and my overactive protective barrier blocking them all along. I began work on changing this straightaway. I will admit, though, I have found it very hard, probably the hardest change to make so far, and am still working on it as it sneaks back in there if I'm not careful. I have had to force myself to look directly at people and be mindful of my body language to retrain myself. I am pleased to say that Nadur has not found it necessary to show me this one again.

He has made it very clear that he doesn't tolerate egos, though. If anybody comes near who has an ego problem, Nadur visibly changes; I see it in his eyes, his demeanour, and then his actions. He mirrors the person, and very quickly a battle ensues. He can't drop it; it's so wrong to him that he gets very angry about it. I have had to change my farrier and other equine professionals to ones who have no ego because Nadur will not work with those who have an ego. Nadur has shown me other things too; one of these is something that I think a lot of people struggle with.

# CHAPTER 21

# TRUST

In the field, Nadur began coming over to me, getting right up into my space, head in the air, and demanding neck massages—clearly overstepping the boundaries we had worked on. It almost felt that he was challenging me to something other than dominance. He was definitely doing something more than just wanting a massage or scratch. Still, it was uncomfortable, so I would move him away out of my space. He would canter off, squeal, and chase Rosa my dog. The whole thing would start again. And the next day would be the same. When I tried to break it down, to make sense of it, I couldn't help but feel that I couldn't trust him 100 per cent, thinking he might resort to old ways by jumping on me or trying to push me about and take control. Unfair, really, as we had moved on from all that years ago. And anyway, this felt different somehow. Trust. Was this about my trust issues then? Particularly with male figures wanting to push me around and control me, taking my newfound self-confidence away? I will simply not go there again; instead, I just walk away from it, not even entertaining the thought. I am not prepared to have to give away any part of myself again for someone else's gain. Was this what was happening though? Was Nadur challenging me to rethink this, to really trust him with every little part of me, to 100 per cent trust him without the need to lose anything? In my life previously, with all my emotional baggage and learned behaviours, it had always been the same: to trust inevitably meant I would lose out. It would start with losing my right to have a choice in things. This would usually lead to my having no voice or any opinion that mattered. Worse still, I then discovered that no one had my back either. And the support I thought I could rely on was fickle; it was an illusion, and could disappear in a moment. Ultimately, I lost confidence in myself and my choices.

I tentatively tested this theory by allowing Nadur in, up close and personal, the next time he challenged me. It was very hard for me to do this, but I welcomed him in close, gave him my whole being, and trusted him, really trusted him, for the first time not to take advantage. I wrapped my arms around him and asked him to help me. I thanked him and just trusted him. He simply relaxed in my embrace. We stood like that for ages with no battles of who was in control, who could take what from the situation. We just stood there as equals in mutual respect and utter calmness. It was magical. I was quite overwhelmed with relief at having taken that step. It felt right and good. I cried a little and also laughed a little. A simple step really, but such a big step in my journey.

This moment made for a profound change deep within me. A few days later, during my next NSA session, I experienced something quite extraordinary. I was lying on the therapy couch face down when I got this fleeting feeling of reaching out for help with my left arm (feminine). In my mind, I found Nadur's big strong neck. I wrapped both arms around it and held on, asking him to help me, just as I had done for real a few days earlier. Briefly, feelings of insecurity and grief hit me, so I just focused on my breathing. I was being really mindful of my breathing out and really feeling it leave my body. Then it was calm, just deep calm. My breathing slowed so much that I didn't feel the need to take in a breath. I was lying there telling myself to take a breath, but I didn't feel the need to take a breath. At first I was a little alarmed, but then I started to wonder how long I could feel like this before I needed to take a breath. It appeared to be endless. There was no panic or feeling of running out of air; it actually felt nice. It was a nice calm place, low and comfy and still. I took a breath eventually only because logic told me it was best to breathe. I didn't feel I needed to though. I have often wondered just how long I could have lain there in that beautiful calm state without taking a breath.

I have since learned that it is an actual thing! People who meditate and become well established in mindfulness of breathing can experience the breath becoming more and more subtle—serene and tranquil. The body becomes so calm, ceasing to feel fatigue, that it seems breathing has become unnecessary. This can be slightly alarming as I found out, but actually the breathing continues, just in a very delicate and subtle form. It is at this point that the mind is free from the five hindrances: desire, anger, drowsiness, restlessness, and doubt. A person in this state is truly calm. It is a wonderful, peaceful feeling. I hope someday I can make it back there and really appreciate it for what it is.

This wonderful, clever horse of mine was giving me the opportunity to learn how to let go of the old patterns of mistrust and learn to safely trust. He was helping me understand that to trust didn't necessarily mean to lose a part of me or get taken advantage of. He once again had helped me to see the pattern I needed to change and then held my hand as I took baby steps towards changing it. In doing so, I found a calmness that I had never experienced before. It seems that deep inside my being, that calmness has remained to this day. I feel calm as if the struggle has left me. That underlying feeling of never quite fitting in has gone. I feel safe. In fact, just the other day I went to see a client whom I hadn't seen for some months. She has the extraordinary ability to see energy. She is a wonderful, insightful woman whom I always enjoy meeting and discussing life with. As I walked towards the stables with her, she looked at me and asked, "What is different? What has changed? Are you seeing someone?"

I said, "What do you mean?"

She said, "The minute I saw you, I could see a change in your energy. You are different, grounded, and whole. You look younger and happier. Have you found a new partner? Are you having sex?" Then she laughed out loud. I burst out laughing with her and then explained about NSA and how my horse was helping me. She was so amazed at my transformation that she demanded the contact details for NSA with the idea of going herself.

Looking back, I realise that I had become quite the control freak myself in my efforts not to allow myself to be controlled. I wasn't being flexible in my thoughts or actions, and I was very determined to prove to myself that I had to go it alone. I didn't need anyone to come along and mess up all my hard work. And it had been hard work to get my life back on track and learn so much about myself. I had become greatly convinced that I would unwittingly end up back where I started years before if I were to allow people in and trust them. So I simply didn't go there. I also became unbalanced in my masculine and feminine energies and had taken a more masculine approach to life. I don't mean in a dressing and behaving like a man kind of way. Although I do recall my young daughter and her friend laughing at the way I was walking down the street in front of them one day. "Mum, you walk like a man!" She laughed, promptly demonstrating a much exaggerated ape-like walk that caused us all to roll around laughing. I did make an effort to walk in a more feminine way after that. What I mean by a masculine approach is that I became more action-orientated and more independent in my thinking and planning. I took on both roles and became dependent upon myself alone, trusting only myself and no one else, losing some of the gentler, more creative aspects. Prior to Nancy's coming into my life, I had unwittingly put myself in male-dominated scenarios all my adult life: agricultural college, the Australian outback, farming in the UK, and the retail business. Also, in having a husband who controlled me but didn't support me, I developed a plethora of behavioural patterns, shutting down my emotions and becoming more masculine in my approach to survive life, protect myself, and prove myself worthy to everyone, including myself. Nancy began the transformation in me, but Nadur insisted I go within and see what was really going on. As I have worked at understanding this and making changes, a lot of grief and fear have surfaced. Fear of what? I don't know! Losing control of my weirdly comforting but fragile and destructive patterns? Showing my hidden, more vulnerable feminine side? Maybe. Nadur has guided me through the seeing of these and the understanding of these. NSA has allowed my body to release unnecessary pain, along with a heap of emotional baggage I had been carrying around, and change has occurred. I no longer have the crippling pain. Nadur has taught me how to allow us both to be who we are and to feel strong in that. I don't have anything to prove to myself or others. Yes, it's nice to have skills to cope with all sorts of things that come up, mechanically, domestically, and outdoors with livestock, etc., but I can still ask for help. It's OK to ask for help or support or to let someone else offer to do something for me. It is also OK to be a middle-aged blonde woman prone to senior moments and all sorts of silliness. It's OK to be me. I am unapologetic for being happy to be me now. I get things wrong and do such stupid things some days that I wonder if it's safe for me to be out alone! But this just makes me laugh at myself now. After all, I'm human, a perfect imperfect human. I work at having a balance in masculinity and femininity and can trust myself not to allow others to control me or take my voice. Nadur supports me in so many ways. He does not take over when I trust him. I have had to establish boundaries with Nadur because he will push me and dominate if the boundaries blur, but this doesn't mean I cannot trust him. This also mirrors the fact that I can maintain certain boundaries for myself, so I feel able to trust without giving up everything. This has been a confusing part of my journey, and has taken me awhile to really understand the differences between control and boundaries, between trust and giving too much. I am still a student in it and continue to work on it, but at least I don't walk like an ape now!

CHAPTER 22

# FOCUS AND FEEL

When I was out in Australia jillarooing, I watched with awe as the eldest son of the family began to work on some unbacked horses. He worked with them in a way I had not seen done before. To my inexperienced nineteen-year-old self, it looked as if the horses loved him every bit as much as he clearly loved them. He would walk into the corral and, I swear to you, they would all turn to face him and stand eagerly waiting, hoping that it was their turn to be picked and taken out to spend time with him. I had never seen horses behave like this. When he asked me to assist him one day, I jumped at the chance. He needed a jockey to just sit on the horse, nothing else— just sit, and he would do the rest. The horse he then presented me was one I knew he had had for only a week, and when it came it was wild—young and literally unhandled. I almost turned and ran, but he assured me I would be safe. He was right, of course. As I sat there, I realised that for the first time I could feel the horse moving freely underneath me—no stiffness, or tension, just relaxed with free movement. The horse really was not bothered at all by the fact that a human was now sitting upon its back for the first time. There was no bucking or trying to run away, just calm acceptance. It was just lovely. I would spend as much time as my work allowed watching this young man work these horses, and I could see how the trust he built was the foundation of their wanting to be with him. He was quiet and gentle and worked in a way the horses clearly understood, so they never got upset or anxious. In fact, they became more willing and expressive the more time he spent with them. When he rode his own horse for the first time after being away from home for two years, I couldn't believe my eyes. He did some in-hand groundwork with it first and then vaulted on—no saddle, no bridle, just a thin rope round its neck like a necklace. He then performed high-level dressage manoeuvres around the open yard, galloped and did sliding stops, spun on a sixpence, and then walked calmly back to the corral. All that after two years of the horse's not being ridden, of horse and human not seeing each other. They were very connected. I couldn't see how the horse was being asked to do it either, it was so subtle. I so wanted to ride like that. It was effortless and beautiful; both human and horse were enjoying themselves. I remember telling myself, *This is how I want to be with horses.* It was magical. I didn't know at the time, but I had just witnessed vaquero horsemanship in motion for the first time. Two years ago I found it again when I went to watch a clinic held by Jeff Sanders, a sixth-generation Californian vaquero. It set me on a path to learn to ride this way with Nadur. Not many people in the UK do it or teach it, so mostly I watch DVDs and go to clinics held by visiting vaquero masters such as Jeff Sanders and the wonderful horseman Stephen Halfpenny when he visits from Australia. I read, I watch, and then I just have a go. Nadur, being so sensitive, makes it clear when I get things right and when I get it wrong, He is very clever, too clever for his own good sometimes, and when coupled with such a novice person as me, he can fake things, such as not properly stepping through with his left hind foot and making it seem that he is doing so, only to turn around and not quite do it at the last minute! We have a lot of fun and I find this amusing rather than annoying. To me it shows how much he uses his brain to work things out. I'm lucky to have no pressures with him, no time restraints, no competition record to create, and no personal goal to reach. It's all about the journey with him. It's about me listening to the lessons he has for me and having a nice time with him.

Underlying all of it, though, is the lesson on focus that I find myself in currently—really learning to focus in the moment and internally. Horses are masters of distraction. When I'm working with horses doing bodywork, it amuses me constantly the many ways they will try to distract me from what I am doing, particularly when I find an area they don't want me to go. They try to convince me there is something terribly important to look at outside, or they will pretend something scary has come into the yard. As long as I stay focused on what it is I am doing, those terribly important and scary things are suddenly no longer important or scary. It is the same when I'm riding Nadur. To stay truly focused on what I want translates simply to controlling my thoughts and not getting distracted by other thoughts. It also means I must be careful of what I tell myself. For example, I would tell myself that I *was* going to have gentle, soft hands when riding, which translates to *I have rigid hands right now!*

Nadur makes it apparent when I'm not truly focused or when I'm focusing on the wrong things. He squeals his disapproval at me or shakes his head violently and stamps his feet. Initially, I would think this was just bad temper. However, I have evolved to understand that he is communicating his feelings towards what I am doing, and it always results in my realising that I am not truly focused on the task at hand. I am confusing him or annoying him with my incongruences. I regularly need to address these. When I do, he is utterly amazing. He is a great motivator to improve myself.

Every time I think, *I've got this,* Nadur shows me there is more I can do. It's about everything I do. Such as the lesson he taught me about noticing the tiny test he would perform by moving his feet. I missed these little tests initially and paid the price. Once I started to notice the tiny tests, I progressed. The same applies now. Once I started to focus on the tiny thoughts and disallowed any thought to go unnoticed, I progressed! Stephen Halfpenny took my hand during a clinic and said, "Helen, you are nice and soft in your hands, but you are like a rock in your elbow. You need to be soft in your whole arm, your whole body." I remember just looking at him dumbfounded for a few seconds and then laughing at myself loudly. Two things came to mind: Remember, I had been telling myself that I had gentle, soft hands when riding, and voilà, that is what I had. I had forgotten about the rest of my body, however. Also, weeks earlier Kelly May and I had been hacking out together, and she had been trying to get me to control my elbows. Even though I ended up saying aloud what I wanted them to do, they seemed to be doing their own thing, as if they didn't belong to my body at all. It made us laugh a whole bunch, but it also highlighted that I never thought about my elbows or felt them as part of me. Now it appears this lesson applies to the rest of my body too.

I straight-away started riding around the arena, imagining my body to be like Mr Soft's, if you remember that advert for Trebor Softmints, really feeling all of me and trying to soften every part of me. Then quickly I decided that I could well start looking pale and completely boneless if I were to focus on that too much, so I changed it to just having no resistance in my body. Nadur immediately rewarded this focus and mindful body awareness with the most amazing trot I had ever felt from him. There was no resistance in either of us!

It was the moment I began to understand how important it is to be *in* my body, not *out* of my body. I began to realise that this is not just about when I am riding but that it applies to everything I do. I have spent years being outside my body, sort of dissociated from it, living in the outside world and not paying attention to the inside. Nadur is teaching me to be present within my body. He has focused my attention to my insides, and in doing so I feel different in myself. I used to feel as if I were part of a play, acting out a role in someone else's story, walking in someone else's shoes that didn't quite fit, all the time ignoring the uncomfortable clues, until I didn't know who

I was any more, who I really was. With Nadur nudging me in the right direction, and with my having experiences such as the mindful breathing, where I was absolutely immersed inside myself, exploring the feeling of not needing to breathe, I am reconnecting to me, the inside me, more and more. I am walking in my own boots now in my own story, and it feels very good.

Nadur does not tolerate lack of focus from me. He sees the potential in me, and he demands my best at all times. He will be, and does still appear, intimidating at times, making it clear when he feels I need to up my game. Although this is frustrating, it makes him honest. There have been many times in our journey together when I have sat down feeling defeated and beaten emotionally and physically by him. I have ranted, swearing I am going to give up horses completely, swearing that I am going to sell him and be done with his attitude. Then, with my rant exhausted, my stubborn side has kicked in and I have gone back to the task at hand with a determination and focus that Nadur has accepted as appropriate. In return, he has given his best and has left me speechless and ecstatic. Each time I think I can't possibly up my game any more, he proves me wrong. Nadur and Stephen helped me to find a new level of lightness that I can't even begin to describe. All I know is that I thought I was light in hand when riding Nadur, doing groundwork with him, or even just leading him from the field. However, this new lightness has actually permeated into everything I do in all aspects of my life, not just when I'm with Nadur; it's as if all of me has softened permanently, not just my hands, elbows, and body, but my whole being. I can only describe it as feeling no resistance in my mind to block the flow of life. My bodywork with horses has become deeper, and it feels as if my softness melts into their bodies and they soften and release tension quicker. I feel privileged to feel this, to have found this softness with their help. To soften so much and flow with everything, be it an animal or just life, well, I find that everything just seems easier. I now feel the tiniest changes in the horses' bodies when I'm working with them and can help them to let go of the tension that is held deeper within their bodies and also within their minds. It must look like I'm doing nothing sometimes, a bit like that reiki woman years ago whom I thought was just standing there next to Nancy, seemingly doing nothing. How far I have travelled—and the things I have learned. I wish everyone could feel like this, could feel the subtle connections between human and horse, could listen and pay attention to all the little things they have to tell us. I must have been shouting all the time to my previous horses with my body language and lack of feel before I learned all these lessons; it must have been very frustrating for them. I feel privileged to be here, at this stage of my journey, enjoying this moment for what it is. I am looking forward to whatever is next, as I'm sure there is so much more to learn. Nadur has not finished with me yet. In fact, I must tell you that it was Nadur who told me to write this book.

CHAPTER 23

# MESSAGES

A friend of mine had arranged for the extraordinary animal communicator Sara Coppin to come out to see her horses. One of these horses had been sold prior to Sara's visit though, and my friend suggested that Sara come to see Nadur in place of that horse. Sara's visit was greatly anticipated because her reputation precedes her. We share clients, so we cross paths in a sense, but I had never met her. It was such fun to hear from Nadur all that he wanted to say. He quite literally wouldn't shut up. Sara had to keep asking him to be patient. There were so many useful, insightful things I got from that visit, and Sara was able to give me answers to my questions about current and past events. We had such a laugh. Some things I didn't fully understand at that moment, but I came to understand them a few months later. For example, I had just put some small jumps out in the school around this time to start Nadur's jumping education but hadn't begun yet as he had hurt his legs in the field. He told Sara to tell me that I could forget all that jumping stuff, saying he wasn't interested, that he was a dancing horse and a very good one! My heart sank as I love jumping and had spent years galloping

cross-country and jumping with a huge smile on my face. *Oh well,*
I thought, *I'm going to have to change my expectations on that front.*

A few months later I was introduced to the *garrocha* by Stephen
Halfpenny. The garrocha is a three-to-four-meter-long pole that
the vaqueros (Spanish cowboys) used to work the bulls with. They
would drag the pole along the ground to deflect the bull's attention
away from their horse's body seemingly athletically, dancing around
the bull to avoid injury. They would also poke the bulls with the
sharper end of the garrocha to move them or knock them over. This
requires high-level classical riding skills, all one-handed, without
dropping the garrocha. To watch a rider dancing with his or her
horse and a garrocha is just beautiful. It's a demonstration of the
highest and, more important, *lightest* form of riding I have ever seen.

It was the last day of a four-day clinic, and my head was exploding
with all the revelations and general awesomeness of the clinic such
that I didn't want to overload my brain with yet another new thing,
but Stephen insisted I try it. Although I only walked in circles
with the garrocha, I had time to feel the difference it made to my
own posture. More importantly, the sudden change I felt in Nadur
underneath me shocked me the most. His body changed; it was as
if he recognised what we were doing—and he was brilliant. I knew
straightaway that this was what he meant by being a dancing horse.
I could feel it in him that this was what he wanted to do. So once
we got home from the clinic and I had time to investigate, I finally
bought a tepee pole. There are not many garrochas in England, I
discovered, so the next best thing is a tepee pole, made of strong but
lightweight Douglas fir and hand-stripped to prevent splinters—
perfect. I chose the one I thought would do the job. As soon as I got
it home, I began the groundwork lessons with it, without Nadur. I
needed training first in the hand positions and manoeuvres, etc.,
before playing around with it with Nadur.

We are continuing to learn and discover the world of the garrocha
together, and it is super exciting. It is a superb tool for correcting my
posture when riding and developing my focus. It's amazing when

the potential for injury is present how it sharpens my focus and concentration. I strongly recommend it to every rider.

However, going back to Sara Coppin's visit, two things came up that surprised me that I would like to share. The first was about my daughter's injury. "Nadur was sending your daughter healing as she had injured her left shoulder and he wanted to know if it was feeling better," Sara said. I had no idea what Nadur was talking about. When I phoned my daughter later and asked her about it, she laughed and said, "*Yes*, it is much better, actually, so can you thank Nadur for me, please?" My daughter was away at university, where she played rugby, and unbeknown to me she had injured her shoulder the week before in a tough match. She had visited Nadur a few days prior to Sara's visit. I couldn't believe it. My horse was aware of my daughter's health before I was. And not only that, but also he was able to help heal her. What a wonderful thing.

The second thing that surprised me was about me writing this book. Nadur wanted to make it very clear that I must write a book about my journey that began with Nancy and is continuing with him. It was very important to him that I know this.

I was out to supper that evening at a dear friend's house, and this message was fortified by an impromptu tarot reading by a lovely woman whom I had never met before. It was a fabulous evening with much laughter. After supper, Angelina got her tarot cards out. Wow, what an amazing experience that was. I had never had a card reading before. During my reading, she summed me up perfectly. She really saw me, my true character and traits. She talked about all the shit I'd been through and then proceeded to accurately talk about things happening presently, decisions and possibilities that were current in my life. She said that I should write a book! *Bloody hell, not her as well!* I thought. At the end of the evening, after doing readings for the others, she looked at me and said, "Right, let's sort you out." She laid her cards out in a different pattern this time, then smiled, pointed at the cards, and said, "Look, three aces! You have to write your book now. Don't delay. You must start writing now." I couldn't believe that twice in the same day I had been told to write this book. So here it is. Who am I to argue with the universe—or Nadur for that matter? He is always right!

CHAPTER 24

# THE ROOT CAUSE

Making sense of and allowing the changes to my physical and emotional self, but also opening my mind enough to allow for changes in my understanding and beliefs, has taken me more than ten years to do. To really address this ability—to allow myself to be ignored and made to feel worthless—has taken a lot of hard lessons and frequent pauses to process those lessons. Just the other day I was slammed on my butt in a stable by a client's horse. I knew it was the universe's way of saying, *Listen up, you have not addressed the root cause yet.* Whilst working with a lovely horse, I lost my balance, got my boots stuck in the rutted rubber mats, and ended up falling backwards, to land heavily on my butt. It was a concussive force that rattled my teeth and stunned me for a moment or two. The horrified owner helped me slowly get to my feet. I knew I was OK structurally, but I was overwhelmed by the fact that once again I had found myself experiencing the same lower back and pelvic pain that always stopped me in my tracks. This was not a coincidence or a random physical occurrence; that would have been the easy explanation, to allow the old me to ignore the actual lesson. No, this was my wake-up call to address some deeper emotional stuff that I clearly had been dancing around for some months now.

I went to see Fran in a NSA session, and sure enough she agreed that the universe can be quite blunt and sometimes painful in its demands that we pay attention. During the session, as she helped my body release the tension from the jaw-shattering, spine-crunching incident, I started to have memories of what I call my "childhood mini traumas". I grew up with loving, caring parents and three siblings, thinking my family were pretty normal. However, I realise now that every life is difficult in its own way. It is not just big physical or emotional traumas that leave behind lasting effects. These childhood mini traumas are not traumas on the scale of abuse and neglect, but they are incidents that, for me, began the process of building the beliefs in my young brain that shaped my life. They are incidents that definitely made a significant emotional impact on my life and on how I subsequently processed further incidents that echoed them. Some were as simple as having all my long blonde hair cut off against my wishes as a four-year-old. This was not done in an intentional way to emotionally harm me; there were valid reasons for it. But at my young age, it had a dramatic effect on how I viewed myself from then on. I was not a little girl any more but looked more like a little boy. Followed by the cruel comments fellow pupils made the next day at school, I found that being in the spotlight was not a pleasant experience. I remember wanting to run and hide away but not being able to. The first school I went to at four years old, in the 1970s, was in South Wales, and to speak English in school time was prohibited. English was our first language though, so unintentionally, in my enthusiasm to learn, I would ask questions in English, only to be told off vehemently and given lines of "You must not speak English" and "You must write it out over and over in Welsh." I was four, for goodness' sake! Eventually, fearful of the humiliation and condemnation of being English, being different, I stopped asking questions and became very shy and quiet in class. I stopped putting myself in the firing line. This was the start of my pervasive sense of fear, particularly in groups of people—fear of rejection or humiliation. Getting along with other kids was hard; I felt that I didn't fit. Living in a tiny Welsh village, I seldom had friends round to play. It was just the four of us siblings together most of the time. Growing up in the 1970s also meant living under very strict rules, handed down to my parents from their parents. Children should be seen and not heard is the greatest of these. A good example of this in my family is the day I was playing in my grandparents' garden, spinning around and making myself dizzy with my arms outstretched to the sides. I then wobbled sideways when I stopped spinning and promptly fell into a rose bush. My right arm fell between two large, thick, very thorny branches and became impaled. I couldn't move. I was trapped, and it really bloody hurt. The shock of my situation saw me open my mouth and scream for help. My grandfather came out of the house, walked over to me, and in his authoritative schoolteacher voice shouted, "Stop that stupid noise right now!" I did shut up immediately, so it was very effective, but again in my head it was another lesson in not to show my true feelings. I internalised the message that it is wrong to make a fuss and is stupid to feel like that. My grandfather did disentangle me from the rose bush and take me inside to get the thorns taken out of my arm because he was a lovely man and I adored him. What's interesting is that I never thought of this incident until it came up in my NSA sessions, which is when I discovered the impact it obviously had made on my young mind. I saw how it was part of the development of my brain's way of coping with shock and injury. As we have seen earlier, I stay quiet, do not make a fuss, and carry on.

There were lots of rules in our house—and for good reason. We were four young kids, and as my father worked away during the week, my mum had to cope on her own. I remember her relentlessly boiling terry towelling nappies, cleaning, and cooking. There were no fancy washing machines, dishwashers, or disposable nappies to help in those days. She had a wooden spoon that became the threat to keep us in line—seldom used, I might add, but the threat was there all the same. It was the 1970s, remember. That wooden spoon, cracked across your legs or rapped across your knuckles, was a good reminder to stay quiet and to refrain from provoking Mum or displeasing her. As long as I played within the rules, conducted myself within the rules at the dinner table, and didn't cause an upset, I could stay under the radar of the wooden spoon. So keeping my feelings and opinions to myself was becoming automatic. I recently realised how powerful these rules have been in shaping my own opinions. Even the family dog had rules to live by. Years later, when I was in my forties and had my own home, getting another dog myself, I realised I was still applying my parents' rules to how I was keeping her—not on sofas, not upstairs, and not on the beds. I must say that it was quite liberating, too, to break those rules and have my dog snuggle up with me.

When we moved from Wales to the haunted house in England, this underlying sense of fear of ridicule and the growing pattern of keeping quiet so as not to make a fuss brought real *fear* for my safety to the forefront, but without the ability to understand it. I did not feel safe in that house; I felt as if I could be hurt at any moment by something I couldn't explain or see. I could feel the resentment, the dislike, and the potential for harm, but I couldn't see where it was coming from. It was imminent but secret. It was strong, powerful, and everywhere, in every room and out in the garden. In fact, one day in the garden, all four of us were playing in between three trees which had been planted in a triangle close together, forming the perfect tree house. I recall being very happy. We were laughing loudly at something my youngest brother had just done, when suddenly we all stopped abruptly. We stopped laughing at the exact same moment, saying nothing to each other, and then all turned like a flock of starlings in formation and ran together towards the kitchen door. As we ran into the house, my mum startled and said, "What on earth are you all doing? It's sunny out there. Go outside and play."

One of us answered for all of us: "We are not allowed out there any more. We have to be quiet." She asked us who had told us that.

We looked at each other quizzically. We didn't know how we knew; we just knew. And we had all received the same message at the same time without its being said aloud. One of us must have tried to explain, and we were told by Mum, "Don't be so silly. Don't be so daft. There is no such thing." We were afraid to go back outside, and we must have looked it too because she let us stay inside to play even though it was sunny—usually unheard of. Again, Mum was trying to put us at ease with her comments, making light of the situation, because clearly we were all scared, but in my mind her behaviour reinforced my thoughts of, *Don't make a fuss. Your opinion/feelings are wrong.* So we didn't talk about things, Mum and Dad did not talk about things, and I didn't say how I really felt. I'm a sensitive, so the fear was very real to me, but if there was no such thing out there telling me and my siblings not to stay outside, then why did I feel like this? I was really scared and I didn't feel safe, but no one else seemed too bothered about that. I was terrified at night, preferring to be sick in my bedroom and thereby risking upsetting my parents than to go out onto the landing and run to the bathroom.

These and other childhood mini traumas shaped my beliefs and behaviours. As a result, I became unable to assert my true self. As I got older, I had to cope with a bullying problem in secondary school, and I quickly withdrew from being good at stuff such as sports and music. It was safer to stay quiet, unseen, and out of view. Staying out of the limelight was safer. Unfortunately, having to wear a brace later, when I was thirteen years old, brought me so much into the unwanted, unpleasant limelight that I developed anxiety. I was then ridiculed mercilessly for my anxiety twitches and flinches, the eczema that burst out on my eyes, making my eyelashes fall out, and the skin red, raw, and sore from itching. Add to this the "buck teeth" and "goofy" comments, and you see I became shyer and shyer and starting skipping lessons. I felt very uncomfortable in my own skin, as if it didn't fit, couldn't fit. I couldn't even escape the ridicule at home. Eventually, at eighteen years old, I jumped on a plane and flew to Australia. I escaped. I went as far away as possible. Although at the time and for many years later I didn't realise that this was exactly what I had done, I can see it now. I never thought of my childhood as traumatic or unusual, but now I see the growing effect the mini traumas had on shaping my beliefs and on what I subsequently kept attracting into my life. I had difficulty standing up for myself as an adult, adopting a "just go along with it" attitude even if I really didn't want to. Running away from myself to Australia, straight into a job that had me needing to prove to myself that I was every bit as good as the others, was the start of the repetitive patterns that I can now identify. I came home and went straight into agricultural college, and then into a marriage to a fundamentally nice guy, but a guy with his own issues and his own belief system that would keep my negative beliefs about myself alive. I always had interpreted his actions as being directed against me, not understanding that they came from his own insecurities. But everything always comes back to the reality that I did not feel at home in my own skin for years, especially when I had to stick my head above the parapet of my comfort zone or believe in myself. To stay quiet, hidden, and out of the limelight became my sole objective and so that is exactly what I attracted into my life. It became so ingrained that I shied away from groups and parties. Even walking into a pub on my own was a no-go.

Finally, Nancy opened my mind up to change. Jacko supported and healed me, and Nadur is showing me the remaining core beliefs and patterns that I need to address.

I feel what I feel, and I know what I know, and nobody can ever tell me otherwise because I am the only one who knows how I feel or what I know at any given time.

I developed beliefs from my own interpretations of events, developed patterns of behaviour and coping mechanisms to survive with those beliefs, and continuously attracted more of the same types of events and people into my life to reaffirm those beliefs. I had to get control of my thoughts and emotions and direct them more appropriately to attract different things into my life. I had to discover and see my behaviours and coping patterns if I was to be able to change them and then begin to understand where my beliefs came from in the first place. Only once I did this was I able to change my perspective of events, from blaming others with "My whole life seems to see me in situations surrounded by people who constantly undermine my self-worth and my confidence" to saying, "It is all my doing, my own creation, and my own interpretation."

Taking responsibility for all my choices and experiences has allowed me to develop a healthier opinion of myself. The ridding my body of the physical pain caused by emotional trauma stuck in my body and the learning of how my brain functions and how to use it in a healthier way all began on that day as I stood there looking at that most delicious chocolate-brown bay mare called Nancy.

## The Whole Truth

Now that I have taken ownership of my journey, what once was comfortable to me now feels very unfamiliar and wrong. I navigate by how I feel, staying firmly on the path I choose and not the path my subconscious chooses. I try to incorporate brain science into everyday life and allow life to unfold without force. I achieve this with the extraordinary guidance of my horse Nadur. I am happy every day, and I love everything and every animal and/or human I come into contact with each day. I am grateful for my health, my family, and my human and animal friends. I am wealthy in more ways than I ever thought possible, and I actively enjoy thinking up my future.

Although I began writing this book with the intention of being honest about and true to all the weird and wonderful events with my horses that have led me to this point, I was still finding it hard to write about some of the more "out there" or more unusual things that I have encountered. This is because of the sceptical conditioned mindset I developed through life but also because of the great deal of time I have spent feeling alone in this magical world of horsey healing and learning. I have tested the waters, as it were, on some of my clients and friends over the years, talking about some of my experiences and have been met with all sorts of responses, from really interested and curious to absolute denial and disbelief. On several occasions, the responses were so extreme that I lost clients and friendships—people who clearly thought I was deranged and not stable enough to be around! That made me very cautious about discussing some of this stuff at all. But over the years of learning and growing, and particularly since doing NSA, I see that it was their lack of knowledge and self-development within the constraints of society's conditioning that made them react as they did. That is their problem to solve, not mine. I shouldn't let it stop me from sharing with others what I have experienced and learned. I still, however, do feel marooned some of the time, until today. Today I watched a horsemanship summit online that brought together horsemen and horsewomen from all over the world to share their knowledge with us. There were bodyworkers, trainers, behaviourists, and communicators. It was a glorious conglomeration of kind, empathic horsemanship styles and techniques that everyone and anyone could learn from and use. The one thing in common with all the presenters, however, was a deep, absolute knowing that lightness and soft hands, and mindfulness, are the key to truly being with a horse. There are many facets to this. I was thrilled and blown away at the same time by how many people are out there, people like me, who have experienced similar things with their horses and have then taken this change of events and run with it, unabashed and unashamed, not being held back or quieted by the conditioning of society. I am not alone. *I am not alone.* What a wonderful feeling. I watched hours of footage from these awesome people—some I knew, some I had never heard of—and it gave me the confidence to get this book written and remain true to my goal of being honest and candid about every experience, not leaving any of it out. There are a lot of people out there who possibly have felt alone or do feel alone in their quest to go down a different route with horses, be it the tack they use or the way they work with their horses, or just the philosophies behind it all. I feel that a change is coming, that a tide is turning—and it's a tide that anyone can ride with any horse of any age or breed or discipline. It's about having another option that doesn't involve spurs, tight nosebands, cruel gadgets, or strength. This helps us know that it's OK to use everything at our disposal to help to understand what our horses are telling us, from communicators, to herbologists, to trainers who teach connection without force.

When I watch horsemen and horsewomen who work with their horses with no rope, or tack, or restraints of any kind, they seem to be very magical. I am beginning to learn that although it is absolutely magical, it most definitely isn't magic. All of us can do this; all of us can learn the horse's language; and all of us can have that magical connection with our own horses. They can heal us, teach us, bring us joy, and carry us through bad times to wonderful times with reciprocal respect and kindness. They just need us to lighten, listen, learn, and be open to changing our own habits and conditioned limitations.

Without a doubt, I would not be where I am now without the healing, strength, and guidance that Nancy and Jacko so willingly gave, helping me to open my mind and grow.

Without a doubt, I would not have been able to go within myself, understand my mind, and change my patterns and beliefs without Nadur. Mental health is such a problem for so many people in the modern world, but our animals can help us; they can show us and guide us and heal us if we listen. My animals are an integral part of my own mental well-being. I will remain mindful of horses forever.

# EPILOGUE

## Is There More Going On?

I have enjoyed the whole process of writing this book. Revisiting these extraordinary events has caused me to understand their lessons better. In a sense, the pieces of the puzzle have all been put in place, lacing together a life-changing journey. I have been truthful and accurate, although at times I wonder the sense in it as this may read like I'm a complete loon. But all this happened exactly as I've written it. I hope that those of my readers out there who have also had some wonderful experiences can find a way to tell the world, for our horses' sake. As I have discovered, they have so much to tell us and teach us if only we watch and listen. What began as an opening of my mind to the unusual and sometimes unexplainable has turned into an exploration of my mental health and physical well-being. My horses have taught me to see the connections between what they show me and what is going on within my own body and mind. The undeniable mirroring of behaviours and restrictions that occurs between horse and human has seen me release emotional and physical trauma from my body. I am free of so much of the unnecessary baggage I was carrying around. My mind has been reconditioned to follow patterns of my choosing. It is healthy and more focused. And yours could be too. I am just an ordinary person. I have neither had any major trauma nor experienced any abuse, but still I retained so much baggage just from life, relationships, and experiences.

So stand back and look and watch your horses. Open your mind to what they may be showing you. What do you see them doing? Take an honest look at yourself and let them help. I marvel at how I met the right people at the right time along my journey once I opened my mind to change. You will too, because the universe provides. I have become very good friends with a lot of these people; I affectionately think of them as my tribe. I am still enjoying my journey of softness with Nadur and will continue on my NSA journey, so I know my tribe will continue to grow.

A train of thought I am mulling over a lot lately has to do with how childhood experiences shape our brain's development and behavioural patterns. Through my dealings with the foster children, I witnessed an array of strange behaviour. I became aware very quickly that they interpreted things quite differently from my daughter. I didn't know then that it was because I was dealing with nervous systems that had developed differently to cope with the trauma—the dangerous or extreme environment these children had been growing up in. Essentially, they were hardwired differently from my daughter and her friends. They couldn't decipher between play-fighting or martial arts training and a genuine threat to their well-being from another person. They also had not had the opportunity to develop a sense of their own abilities or an awareness of their own selves. To climb a tree, paddle in a river, or ride a horse would put them in a spin because they didn't have the necessary trust in their own bodies, and they didn't know their limits or how to interpret the sensations these activities stimulated. They would react much more quickly and escalate into panic at the smallest of things. The worrying thing is that I have witnessed this exact same irrational, unpredictable behaviour in many horses too.

One of my dearest friends, Sara Withy, and I met over eighteen years ago. We became riding buddies. We regularly discuss the wonderful world of horses and all our extraordinary experiences we have had with them. Sara could write a book herself and entertain us all with stories of her wonderful equine friends she has had over the years and the wonderful adventures she had with them, from working shires, to driving Shetlands, to jousting knights' horses. We laugh so much when we are together; it's become our tonic when either of us needs a helping hand. Her herd of horses is usually made up of lost souls who found their way to her after having been deemed worthless/useless or just surplus. She gives them a home, a job, and love. Whisper is one such horse. Initially it was me who had found her. She just appeared one day in my field. My landlord's daughter had sent her to a yard nearby to be sold. They had deemed her unsellable, and therefore she had to be removed from their yard immediately. No more information was forthcoming. I got to know Whisper over the next few weeks. Turns out she was terrified of buckets and not very trusting of people, but other than that, she seemed nice enough. She is a beautiful jet-black Welsh Section D, and her coat shines like an onyx crystal. As I got to know her, I wondered why she had been deemed unsellable as she seemed to be really nice and very sweet. Sara came to see her and fell in love with her. After spending six weeks or so getting to know her, Sara offered Whisper a home within her herd. We came to the conclusion that Whisper had not been backed or started very well, if at all. She didn't seem to understand what she was being asked, but she learned quickly and seemed happy to learn. Over the years, Whisper has displayed very random behaviour for a horse and seems to have limited capacity to learn as if she up and forgets—and you have to start all over again. Or she learns something very well, but when she is introduced to the next logical step, she forgets the basics again, as if she has limited capacity to retain information. She has learned so many things and then acts as if she has no clue what she is supposed to do. Sara, ever so understanding, has given her time and has gently made progress, only to find herself back at square one with a horse that acts like it's a green three-year-old. We have often commented on how if Whisper were human, she would probably have been categorised as autistic or given some other label by now. Even our other horses have found her difficult, at times standing and looking at her as if they too don't understand the behaviour she is displaying at that particular moment. We could be out hacking, and out of the blue Whisper will reverse very fast and double-barrel the nearest horse. Just like the foster kids who had heightened reactions to the smallest of stimuli. She will be tacked up, ready to go, and suddenly rodeo like a bronc horse on the spot when something touches her side. Then she'll stop and go back to chewing and standing with her legs relaxed as if nothing happened. She will walk past a combine harvester in full action then spook violently at a car trying to come past her slowly. She also seems not to know how to behave with other herd members, as if she can't speak their language. This makes her behave quite violently towards them sometimes, but if she is put in a paddock on her own, then she will settle really quickly and relax. Her reactions are so random, and the extent of her reaction so unnecessary, that they are not at all normal for a horse.

It is well-documented that successful brain development leading to normal-functioning adults who react to varying stimuli in a predictable fashion begins with our caregivers when we are very young. An amazing book I have just read, *The Body Keeps the Score*, by Bessel Van der Kolk, gives brilliant insight into how complex our brain function is and how it is paramount to our children's mental health that we be mindful parents. The environment we grow up in and our experiences in our early years shape our brain development to cause us to cope in set ways. Trauma can derail us from the norm at any age, but childhood neglect or abuse sets us up for developing neurological coping patterns of behaviour that seem unnatural to those such as I who were blessed with a nurturing, safe childhood. *The Body Keeps the Score* helped me to understand why I had developed my own patterns of behaviour, which I first had to be made aware of with Nadur's help, then work through and change. Because of repetitive scenarios resulting always in my own interpretation of being unworthy, or feeling less than others and having no right to make a fuss, I had learned to cope by shutting down and developing several behavioural patterns. Some I have discussed in this book; others, I have not. I will say that the very common one of drinking heavily was definitely something I developed and practised for a while. My brain had become programmed to deal with certain stimuli in very set ways. I wasn't even aware of some of these. I want to make it clear that I was not abused or neglected in my childhood and that I had a safe and nurturing home. But I still developed patterns that I now know came from my childhood experiences, these patterns becoming more pronounced as my experiences in adulthood, through the positions I put myself in repeatedly or the things and people I attracted into my life, confirmed what I believed: I was not as worthy as others, I should remain quiet, and I should refrain from making a fuss. So even though I did not have a traumatic childhood, in contrast to the foster kids I worked with, I still developed odd beliefs and coping mechanisms. We all do.

I witnessed foster kids who couldn't deal with people being nice to them. They didn't know how to deal with it because they had not developed the coping mechanisms for such a scenario, so they would act out in panic. Put back into a dangerous, violent, or neglectful environment, they would settle. Even though it was not a safe environment, they could cope better with it than with a safe environment because they had the learned patterns of behaviour to cope with danger, violence, and neglect. A horse I had the pleasure of getting to know for a couple of weeks displayed the exact same tendency. He was fourteen and had been moved from home to home quite a lot. Mostly he was polite, gentle, and seemingly normal, but when he was in a situation that stimulated his sympathetic nervous system, he would panic—and then it was very difficult to get him out of fight or flight mode. I tried everything I knew to calm him, all done in a firm but nonaggressive manner. Then I witnessed his owner deal with it. Her answer was to punch him in his face, whip him with the line or anything else she had to hand, and shout at him.

Unbelievably, he would calm right down and regain brain function very quickly. In my mind, that was not the best environment for a horse, but he could definitely cope with that better than he could cope with me being gentle, quiet, and respectful. I often wondered if over time his response could be reversed as with the children?

Was Whisper displaying behaviour that could have started when she was a foal? Had she been weaned early, and by early I mean under twelve months of age? It is common to wean at six months and to keep weaned foals together instead of with the herd. Is this causing continuous stress? Are they surviving in flight mode and developing behavioural patterns that are not normal for a horse? Is this causing the young foal's brain to develop differently, which shows up as unpredictable behaviour later in life? I have worked with and looked after a lot of horses over the years, and I have seen a lot who cannot be put out with other horses as they attack them. I see a lot of horses who overreact to small stimuli that other horses find quite easy to assimilate as harmless. I see a lot of horses doing the "wall of death" routine in the lunge pen who are definitely in flight mode and not able to respond normally.

To develop normally, safe social interaction is a biological necessity for humans, not an option. The same can be said for horses—herd animals. To segregate them away from a herd environment too early may be doing more damage than we know.

When we decided to put Nancy to foal, my daughter and I had already said that Nancy would choose when to wean Nadur. We would follow her lead. When she began to push him away when he was around a year old, she also began to look a little drained and started to lose weight. This made it easy for us to know it was time to help her wean him. He was never taken away from her, just stabled next to her. For the next couple of months, we stuck to a routine that gave him time during the day to nuzzle and interact with her over the stable door, time out to play with another horse, and time to sleep in the stable whilst Nancy went out for her time to play and exercise. Neither of them got stressed by this, and it gave Nancy time to dry off. They all went back out together when she was ready, and that's how his weaning went—unremarkable and unstressful for both of them. Nadur doesn't overreact to potentially scary stuff; he remains present and in control of his thought processes. He will spook like any horse, but it doesn't trigger an irrational bolt or bucking bronco scenario (which I have witnessed countless horses doing). Even when he is cross about something, such as his mate being turned out without him, he can still behave well and work through it safely without losing his ability to think.

I have so many questions still, such as, how much are our animals really trying to heal us? Remember, Nadur said he had been sending my daughter healing to help her shoulder injury. Well, it got me to thinking of some other cases I had worked on where the possibility that the animals not only had been aware of the state of health of their humans but also may have been trying to heal them, and sometimes to the detriment to their own health. One particular story I want to share with you briefly is of a little dog I was asked to work with. I shall refer to him as O.

Most horsey people have dogs. I was being asked all the time if I could work with the dogs as well as the horses. It made sense to find a course that followed the same principles as the Masterson method in that the dogs have a say and a choice in the matter and lightness is key. Having chosen to train as a Galen canine myotherapist, I completed their diploma course in 2017, giving me the ability to begin working with dogs. O was a young dachshund who had lost the use of his back legs one morning. When I met him for the first time, he was coming towards me up the garden path, full of life and very jolly, but dragging his hind end. It didn't seem to be slowing him down, I noted with a smile, but he had no use of his back legs at all. The vets had said that an operation costing thousands was his only option, and even then it was fifty-fifty that it would give him the use of his legs again. His owners had opted to find another way. Along with anti-inflammatory medication and time, I began working with O (with veterinary permission, of course).

What a bundle of joy. He just loved everything and everyone. His wonderful owners diligently did the strengthening exercises with O and the massage homework I assigned to them every fortnight. This was quite difficult as he was tiny and they were elderly, so bending down for that long was not an option. Thinking outside the box and throwing the rule book out the window, they decided to exercise him by having him walk back and forth across their kitchen table. This was perfect and did make us laugh. O recovered and within four months was running around his garden as if it had never been any different for him. However, a few months later, his human mum quite suddenly and very sadly died of cancer. The coincidence and timing was such that I couldn't help but think, *Had O been trying to heal her or at least show her she was unwell and, because of this, lost the use of his own legs?* Her cancer was in her pelvis! Food for thought, for sure. I am so glad the owner had gotten to see O running around again before she passed, but it gave me a lot to think on. I have started to keep a journal of other equine and canine cases that have similar thought-provoking synopses. Is there more to our animals than we are aware?

# GOOD READS AND INFORMATIVE WEBSITES

**Horse related:**

Mastersonmethod.com – Integrated Equine Performance Bodywork
Markrashid.com – Mark Rashid, Considering the Horse.
Stevehalfpenny.com – Steve Halfpenny, Light Hands Equitation.
Californiabridlehorse.com - Jeff Sanders
Brannaman.com – Buck Brannaman
Cam4animals.co.uk
Animalspirit.org - Anna Breytenbach
'Tao of Eqqus' by Linda Kohanov
'Nod Whispers' by Peter Neilson
'The Horse Boy' by Rupert Issacson
'Tug of War: classical versus "Modern" Dressage' by Dr Gerd Heuschmann
'Ride from the Heart' by Jenny Rolfe

**Mind, Brain and Body:**

'The Genie in your Genes' by Dawson Church Ph.D.
'The Biology of Belief' by Bruce H. Lipton, Ph.D
'The body keeps the score' by Bessel Van Der Kolk
'The secret' by Rhonda Byrne

'The 12 stages of Healing' by Donald M. Epstein D.C with Nathaniel Altman
'You can heal your Life' by Louise L. Hay.
'Heal your Body' by Louise L. Hay
'The Journey' by Brandon Bays

**My Tribe:**

Facebook.com/carolyntyrerartist/
Hedgewitchessentials.co.uk
Abundantlifechiropractic.co.uk
Awakenchiropractic.co.uk
Soul2soul.me
Energyhealinguk on face book
Connectednaturally.co.uk
Cotswoldsveterinaryaccupuncture.co.uk
'Animal Spirit Guides' by Steven D. Farmer, Ph. D
'Animal Speak' by Ted Andrews

Printed in Great Britain
by Amazon